INTRODUCING ISSUES WITH OPPOSING VIEWPOINTS®

Garbage and Recycling

Cynthia A. Bily, *Book Editor*

GREENHAVEN PRESS
A part of Gale, Cengage Learning

GALE
CENGAGE Learning·

Detroit • New York • San Francisco • New Haven, Conn • Waterville, Maine • London

Elizabeth Des Chenes, *Director, Publishing Solutions*

© 2013 Greenhaven Press, a part of Gale, Cengage Learning

Gale and Greenhaven Press are registered trademarks used herein under license.

For more information, contact:
Greenhaven Press
27500 Drake Rd.
Farmington Hills, MI 48331-3535
Or you can visit our Internet site at gale.cengage.com

For product information and technology assistance, contact us at

Gale Customer Support, 1-800-877-4253
For permission to use material from this text or product, submit all requests online at www.cengage.com/permissions

Further permissions questions can be e-mailed to permissionrequest@cengage.com

Articles in Greenhaven Press anthologies are often edited for length to meet page requirements. In addition, original titles of these works are changed to clearly present the main thesis and to explicitly indicate the author's opinion. Every effort is made to ensure that Greenhaven Press accurately reflects the original intent of the authors. Every effort has been made to trace the owners of copyrighted material.

Cover image © Margaret I. Wallace/Shutterstock.com.

LIBRARY OF CONGRESS CATALOGING-IN-PUBLICATION DATA

Garbage and recycling / Cynthia A. Bily, book editor.
   pages cm. -- (Introducing issues with opposing viewpoints)
  Includes bibliographical references and index.
  ISBN 978-0-7377-6277-8 (hardcover)
1. Recycling (Waste, etc.)--United States. 2. Refuse and refuse disposal--Environmental aspects--United States. 3. Plastic scrap--Environmental aspects--United States. I. Bily, Cynthia A.
  TD794.5.G368 2013
  628.4'458--dc23
 	
                                                       2012038277

Printed in the United States of America
1 2 3 4 5 6 7 16 15 14 13

Contents

Chapter 3: How Can Consumers Reduce the Amount of Plastic Waste Generated?

Foreword

Indulging in a wide spectrum of ideas, beliefs, and perspectives is a critical cornerstone of democracy. After all, it is often debates over differences of opinion, such as whether to legalize abortion, how to treat prisoners, or when to enact the death penalty, that shape our society and drive it forward. Such diversity of thought is frequently regarded as the hallmark of a healthy and civilized culture. As the Reverend Clifford Schutjer of the First Congregational Church in Mansfield, Ohio, declared in a 2001 sermon, "Surrounding oneself with only like-minded people, restricting what we listen to or read only to what we find agreeable is irresponsible. Refusing to entertain doubts once we make up our minds is a subtle but deadly form of arrogance." With this advice in mind, Introducing Issues with Opposing Viewpoints books aim to open readers' minds to the critically divergent views that comprise our world's most important debates.

Introducing Issues with Opposing Viewpoints simplifies for students the enormous and often overwhelming mass of material now available via print and electronic media. Collected in every volume is an array of opinions that captures the essence of a particular controversy or topic. Introducing Issues with Opposing Viewpoints books embody the spirit of nineteenth-century journalist Charles A. Dana's axiom: "Fight for your opinions, but do not believe that they contain the whole truth, or the only truth." Absorbing such contrasting opinions teaches students to analyze the strength of an argument and compare it to its opposition. From this process readers can inform and strengthen their own opinions, or be exposed to new information that will change their minds. Introducing Issues with Opposing Viewpoints is a mosaic of different voices. The authors are statesmen, pundits, academics, journalists, corporations, and ordinary people who have felt compelled to share their experiences and ideas in a public forum. Their words have been collected from newspapers, journals, books, speeches, interviews, and the Internet, the fastest growing body of opinionated material in the world.

Introducing Issues with Opposing Viewpoints shares many of the well-known features of its critically acclaimed parent series, Opposing Viewpoints. The articles are presented in a pro/con format, allowing readers to absorb divergent perspectives side by side. Active reading questions preface each viewpoint, requiring the student to approach the material thoughtfully and carefully. Useful charts, graphs, and cartoons supplement each article. A thorough introduction provides readers with crucial background on an issue. An annotated bibliography points the reader toward articles, books, and websites that contain additional information on the topic. An appendix of organizations to contact contains a wide variety of charities, nonprofit organizations, political groups, and private enterprises that each hold a position on the issue at hand. Finally, a comprehensive index allows readers to locate content quickly and efficiently.

Introducing Issues with Opposing Viewpoints is also significantly different from Opposing Viewpoints. As the series title implies, its presentation will help introduce students to the concept of opposing viewpoints and learn to use this material to aid in critical writing and debate. The series' four-color, accessible format makes the books attractive and inviting to readers of all levels. In addition, each viewpoint has been carefully edited to maximize a reader's understanding of the content. Short but thorough viewpoints capture the essence of an argument. A substantial, thought-provoking essay question placed at the end of each viewpoint asks the student to further investigate the issues raised in the viewpoint, compare and contrast two authors' arguments, or consider how one might go about forming an opinion on the topic at hand. Each viewpoint contains sidebars that include at-a-glance information and handy statistics. A Facts About section located in the back of the book further supplies students with relevant facts and figures.

Following in the tradition of the Opposing Viewpoints series, Greenhaven Press continues to provide readers with invaluable exposure to the controversial issues that shape our world. As John Stuart Mill once wrote: "The only way in which a human being can make some approach to knowing the whole of a subject is by hearing what can be said about it by persons of every variety of opinion and studying all modes in which it can be looked at by every character of mind. No wise man ever acquired his wisdom in any mode but this." It is to this principle that Introducing Issues with Opposing Viewpoints books are dedicated.

Introduction

"While all Americans could do more to recycle, we also need to, contrarily, reduce our fixation on it. . . . Recycling gives us permission to consume."

—Susan Burton, "Recycling? Fuhgeddaboudit,"
Mother Jones, May–June 2009

In the summer of 2012, the Boston suburb of Arlington, Massachusetts, joined several other communities in the United States in requiring its residents to recycle part of their household trash. Since September of that year, the town's collection and hauling company has picked up trash from a resident's curb only if it is accompanied by a separate container of materials for recycling. If there is no recycling, the trash is left at the curb. Regular trash in excess of one hundred gallons is not picked up, even if the household has also set out recycling. In a June 14 interview with the *Boston Globe,* Arlington director of public works Michael Rademacher said, "We do feel that there is a certain percentage of the public that doesn't recycle and this will in essence force them to."

Mandatory recycling in large metropolitan areas, including Philadelphia, Seattle, and San Francisco, is driven in part by a concern for the environment. Many people believe that recycling materials like glass, aluminum, steel, and plastic saves energy, reduces greenhouse gas emissions, and leads to less litter. But in Arlington there was also a very practical consideration: The town expects to save money on its bill for waste hauling. Well-established markets for recyclable materials in the Northeast often make it cheaper to separate and sell these materials than to simply haul them away to a landfill or incinerator. And because landfill space in large metropolitan areas is becoming scarce, waste management expenses are increasing even as many city budgets are shrinking. For towns like Arlington and cities like San Francisco—which also requires residents to separate out compostable materials like kitchen scraps and yard waste—recycling is an important part of the plan for handling the large amounts of solid waste that Americans generate each day.

But in other parts of the country, recycling is not cheap; in fact, curbside recycling can cost more than regular trash pickup because of the need for extra trucks and extra stops. In an October 21, 2011, article in the *New York Times*, Mireya Navarro reported that New York City "officials say that it is more expensive to recycle than to send trash to landfills and incinerators for disposal, and that they have to weigh those costs against environmental goals." New York City suspended its curbside recycling program for two years when a budget crisis hit in 2002, and in 2012 it collected only the most common materials, which command a sustainable price on the recyclables market. Yogurt cups, to pick just one often-cited example, are not recyclable through New York City's curbside program—though many other communities do accept them—because the market for that kind of plastic is limited.

Even when a community saves money with recycling, not everyone agrees that it should be required. Steven McClain, posting on the website of the *Somerset County (PA) Daily American* on April 13, 2011, wrote, "Recycling is a conscientious choice someone should make. If they really care about the environment and are concerned, then they will recycle. If not, that is their choice to not do so."

Others, like Susan Burton, who is quoted at the beginning of this introduction, believe that focusing on recycling sidesteps the real issue: Americans are creating ever-growing mountains of soda bottles, junk mail, packaging materials, out-of-style cell phones, take-out containers, grass clippings, and other solid waste—almost five pounds per person per day—and it has to go somewhere. According to the website of the US Environmental Protection Agency, "Nearly everything we do leaves behind some kind of waste." Whether it is buried in a landfill, incinerated in a facility that may or may not generate energy, burned openly in a backyard scrap pile, dumped in the ocean, recycled, or reused, each piece of trash must be dealt with, and Americans often stop thinking about their trash as soon as it hits the garbage can or recycling bin. Many people believe that we have made it so easy to get rid of garbage that we do not consider how much we generate, and that instead of focusing our energy on how to dispose of or recycle our waste, we should concentrate on generating less in the first place.

No one answer will solve the problems of waste disposal in every community. People in cities produce different kinds of waste from people on farms; varying distances from the nearest landfill or incinerator affect the cost of waste disposal; the fluctuating markets for different materials and the availability of recycling facilities determine what can be economically recycled. And while many believe that the best thing to do is to simply consume less, there is increasing pressure on Americans—particularly in this period of economic instability—to put people back to work by consuming more and more.

As city managers, environmentalists, waste disposal companies, scientists, journalists, and student activists work to determine the best ways to deal with municipal solid waste, they must struggle with important questions: How should garbage be disposed of? Is recycling effective? How can consumers reduce the amount of plastic waste generated? The authors of the following viewpoints present a range of answers to these questions.

Chapter 1

How Should Garbage Be Disposed Of?

The disposal of garbage and its effect on the environment is a controversial issue.

Landfills Are Convenient and Environmentally Safe

"Nearly all municipal solid waste landfills (MSWLFs) are required to monitor the underlying groundwater for contamination during their active life and post-closure care period."

US Environmental Protection Agency

In the following viewpoint, the United States Environmental Protection Agency (EPA) describes the landfill methods used in the United States to manage solid waste, more commonly known as "trash" or "garbage." With new guidelines, trash landfills must be built in a way that protects the environment. The viewpoint describes several different requirements a landfill must meet in order to safely and effectively remove waste without damaging the surrounding environment. The EPA is a United States federal government agency that was created to protect human health and the environment.

AS YOU READ, CONSIDER THE FOLLOWING QUESTIONS:
1. According to the author, what is the landfill siting plan?
2. Are municipal solid waste landfills required to monitor underlying groundwater, according to the author?
3. According to the author, what are the three phases of groundwater monitoring requirements?

US Environmental Protection Agency, "Landfills," "Groundwater Monitoring Requirements for Municipal Solid Waste Landfills," and "Closure and Post-closure Care Requirements for Municipal Solid Waste Landfills (MSWLFs)," EPA.gov, July 24, 2012.

Modern landfills are well-engineered facilities that are located, designed, operated, and monitored to ensure compliance with federal regulations. Solid waste landfills must be designed to protect the environment from contaminants which may be present in the solid waste stream. The landfill siting plan—which prevents the siting of landfills in environmentally-sensitive areas—as well as on-site environmental monitoring systems—which monitor for any sign of groundwater contamination and for landfill gas—provide additional safeguards. In addition, many new landfills collect potentially harmful landfill gas emissions and convert the gas into energy. For more information, visit EPA's Landfill Methane Outreach Program.

Municipal solid waste landfills (MSWLFs) receive household waste. MSWLFs can also receive non-hazardous sludge, industrial solid waste, and construction and demolition debris. All MSWLFs must comply with the federal regulations in 40 CFR Part 258 (Subtitle D of RCRA), or equivalent state regulations. Federal MSWLF standards include:

- **Location restrictions**—ensure that landfills are built in suitable geological areas away from faults, wetlands, flood plains, or other restricted areas.
- **Composite liners requirements**—include a flexible membrane (geomembrane) overlaying two feet of compacted clay soil lining the bottom and sides of the landfill, protect groundwater and the underlying soil from leachate releases.
- **Leachate collection and removal systems**—sit on top of the composite liner and remove leachate from the landfill for treatment and disposal.
- **Operating practices**—include compacting and covering waste frequently with several inches of soil [to] help reduce odor; control litter, insects, and rodents; and protect public health.
- **Groundwater monitoring requirements**—require testing groundwater wells to determine whether waste materials have escaped from the landfill.
- **Closure and post-closure care requirements**—include covering landfills and providing long-term care of closed landfills.

- **Corrective action provisions**—control and clean up landfill releases and achieve groundwater protection standards.
- **Financial assurance**—provides funding for environmental protection during and after landfill closure (i.e., closure and post-closure care).

Some materials may be banned from disposal in municipal solid waste landfills including common household items such as paints, cleaners/chemicals, motor oil, batteries, and pesticides. Leftover portions of these products are called household hazardous waste. These

The average American disposes of 4.5 pounds of trash every day. For the country as a whole, this adds up to a total of 250 million tons of garbage a year—much of which ends up in a landfill.

products, if mishandled, can be dangerous to your health and the environment. Many municipal landfills have a household hazardous waste drop-off station for these materials.

MSWLFs can also receive household appliances (also known as white goods) that are no longer needed. Many of these appliances, such as refrigerators or window air conditioners, rely on ozone-depleting refrigerants and their substitutes. MSWLFs have to follow federal disposal procedures for household appliances that use refrigerants. EPA has general information on how refrigerants can damage the ozone layer and consumer information on the specifics of disposing of these appliances.

Groundwater Monitoring Requirements for Municipal Solid Waste Landfills (MSWFs)

Nearly all municipal solid waste landfills (MSWLFs) are required to monitor the underlying groundwater for contamination during their active life and post-closure care period. The exceptions to this requirement are small landfills that receive less than 20 tons of solid waste per day, and facilities that can demonstrate that there is no potential for the migration of hazardous constituents from the unit into the groundwater. All other MSWLFs must comply with the groundwater monitoring requirements found at 40 CFR Part 258, Subpart E–Ground-Water Monitoring and Corrective Action.

To monitor groundwater, facility owners and operators must install a groundwater monitoring system that can collect samples from the uppermost aquifer (defined as the geological formation nearest the natural surface that is capable of yielding significant quantities of groundwater to wells or springs). The groundwater monitoring system consists of a series

> **FAST FACT**
>
> According to the Environmental Industry Associations, there were nearly twenty thousand operating landfills in the United States in 1970, many of them unsafe dumping grounds. Today about nineteen hundred larger, more technologically advanced sanitary landfills handle roughly the same amount of waste.

of wells placed upgradient and downgradient of the MSWLF. The samples from the upgradient wells show the background concentrations of constituents in the groundwater, while the downgradient wells show the extent of groundwater contamination caused by the MSWLF. The required number of wells, spacing, and depth of wells is determined on a site-specific basis based on the aquifer thickness, groundwater flow rate and direction, and the other geologic and hydrogeologic characteristics of the site. All groundwater monitoring systems must be certified by a qualified groundwater scientist and must comply with the sampling and analytical procedures outlined in the regulations. . . .

There are three phases of the groundwater monitoring requirements:

- Detection Monitoring,
- Assessment Monitoring, and
- Corrective Action.

Detection Monitoring

During the detection monitoring phase, MSWLF owner/operators monitor for the 62 constituents listed in Appendix I of 40 CFR Part 258. This consists of sampling at least semiannually throughout the facility's active life and post-closure care period. The frequency of sampling is determined on a site-specific basis by the state regulatory agency.

If at any time during the detection monitoring phase, one of the 62 constituents is detected at a statistically significant higher level than the established background level, the MSWLF owner/operators must notify the state regulatory agency. The facility must establish an assessment monitoring program within 90 days unless the owner/operators can prove that the detection of the constituent(s) was the result of a sampling, analysis, or statistical evaluation error (i.e., a false positive result); a natural fluctuation in groundwater quality; or caused by another source.

Assessment Monitoring

Within 90 days of detecting a statistically significant increase in the constituents listed in Appendix I [of 40 CFR Part 258], a MSWLF must begin an assessment monitoring program. As a first step, samples must be taken from all wells and analyzed for the presence of all 214 constituents listed in Appendix II of 40 CFR Part 258. If any of the constituents listed in Appendix II are detected, the owner/operators must then establish the background levels for these constituents and establish a groundwater protection standard (GWPS) for each. The GWPS represents the maximum allowable constituent level in the groundwater, and is based either on the Safe Drinking Water Act (SDWA) Maximum Contaminant Level (MCL) for that constituent, or the background level of the groundwater at the site if no MCL exists. In cases where the site-specific background level is higher than the MCL, the background level is used for the GWPS.

Within 90 days of establishing the background levels and the GWPS, the owner/operators must then resample for all constituents listed in Appendix I and Appendix II previously detected. Resampling then must be repeated at least semiannually. If none of the Appendix II constituents are found to exceed the GWPS for two consecutive sampling events, the facility may return to the detection monitoring phase. If, however, any of the constituents are detected at a statistically significant level higher than the GWPS, the owner/operators of the MSWLF must characterize the nature of the release, determine if the contamination has migrated beyond the facility boundary, and begin assessing corrective measures.

Corrective Action

Based upon the assessment of corrective measures, a remedy is selected and corrective action begins. Any corrective measure selected must be protective of human health and the environment, meet the GWPS, control the source(s) of the release to prevent further releases, and manage any solid waste generated in accordance with all applicable RCRA regulations. The facility must continue these remedial actions until it has complied with the GWPS for three consecutive years and can demonstrate that all required actions have been completed.

Final Cover Systems

The closure standards for MSWLFs require owner/operators to install a final cover system to minimize infiltration of liquids and soil erosion. The permeability of the final cover must be less than the underlying liner system, but no greater than 1.0 x 10-5 cm/sec. The reason for this requirement is to prevent the "bathtub effect" where liquids infiltrate through the overlying cover system but are contained by a more permeable underlying liner system. This causes the landfill to fill up

Total Municipal Solid Waste Generation

In 2010, the United States generated about 250 million tons of municipal solid waste (MSW).

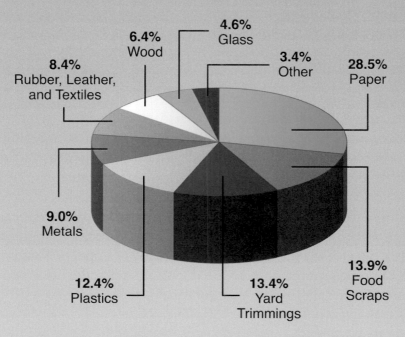

**2010 Total MSW Generation (by Material)
250 Million Tons (Before Recycling)**

4.6% Glass

6.4% Wood

8.4% Rubber, Leather, and Textiles

3.4% Other

28.5% Paper

9.0% Metals

13.9% Food Scraps

12.4% Plastics

13.4% Yard Trimmings

Taken from: EPA, 2012. www.epa.gov/epawaste/nonhaz/municipal/index.htm.

with water (like a bathtub), increasing the hydraulic head on the liner system that can lead to the contaminated liquid (leachate) escaping and contaminating groundwater supplies.

The final cover system must consist of an infiltration layer of at least 18 inches of earthen material covered by an erosion layer of at least 6 inches of earthen material that is capable of sustaining native plant growth. An alternative cover design may be used as long as it provides equivalent protection against infiltration and erosion. Such alternative designs must be approved by the director of an approved/authorized state program.

Closure Plans

Every MSWLF is required to prepare a written closure plan that describes the steps necessary to close the unit in accordance with the closure requirements. This plan must include:

- A description of the final cover design and its installation methods and procedures.
- An estimate of the largest area of the landfill requiring a final cover.
- An estimate of the maximum inventory of waste on site during the landfill's active life.
- A schedule for completing all required closure activities.

Once a MSWLF has received its final shipment of waste, it must begin closure operations within 30 days. A MSWLF, however, may delay closure for up to one year if additional capacity remains. Any further delays after one year require approval from the state director. After beginning, all closure activities must be completed within 180 days (with the exception of an extension from the state director). After closure is complete, the owner/operators then must certify that the closure has been completed in accordance with the official closure plan. This certification must be signed by an independent, registered professional engineer or the state director. At this time, the MSWLF owner/operators also must make a notation on the property deed indicating that the land was used as a landfill and that its future use for other activities is restricted.

Post-Closure Care

Post-closure care activities consist of monitoring and maintaining the waste containment systems and monitoring groundwater to ensure that waste is not escaping and polluting the surrounding environment. The required post-closure care period is 30 years from site closure, but this can be shortened or extended by the director of an approved state program as necessary to ensure protection of human health and the environment.

Specific post-closure care requirements consist of maintaining the integrity and effectiveness of the:

- Final cover system
- Leachate collection system
- Groundwater monitoring system
- Methane gas monitoring system.

The owner/operator of a closed MSWLF must prepare a written post-closure care plan that provides:

- A description of all required monitoring and maintenance activities, including the frequency with which each activity will be performed.
- The name, address, and telephone number of the person to contact during the post-closure care period.
- A description of planned uses of the land during the post-closure care period.

Any use of the land during this period must not disturb the integrity or operation of any of the waste containment systems or the monitoring systems. At the end of the post-closure care period, the owner/operator must certify that the post-closure care has been completed in accordance with the official post-closure care plan. This certification must be signed by an independent, registered professional engineer or the state director. Once signed, the certification is placed in the facility's operating record.

EVALUATING THE AUTHOR'S ARGUMENTS:

The viewpoint you have just read was written by the Environmental Protection Agency (EPA). Members of this agency can be expected to know the environmental aspects of the garbage business very well and to have a deep and clear understanding of the challenges and successes. Do you believe the viewpoint fairly presented these challenges and successes? Why or why not?

Viewpoint 2

Landfills Are Not a Good Long-Term Solution for Waste Disposal

"Unfortunately, landfills leak gaseous, liquid and solid materials."

John D. Halfman

In the following viewpoint John D. Halfman describes the often-overlooked dangers of collecting our garbage and putting it out of sight into landfills. The United States simply generates so much waste, he argues, that handling it all in environmentally friendly ways would cost more than people are willing to pay. Landfills handle many toxic chemicals, and even the most modern landfills experience leaks that cause serious pollution issues, he concludes. Halfman is a professor of geolimnology and hydrogeochemistry and the chair of the Environmental Studies program at Hobart and William Smith Colleges in Geneva, New York.

AS YOU READ, CONSIDER THE FOLLOWING QUESTIONS:
  1. Why, according to the viewpoint, is it difficult to find places to build new landfills in urban areas?
  2. What kinds of hazardous materials are included in the garbage from a typical home, as reported in the viewpoint?
  3. When archaeologists opened a landfill and examined forty-year-old garbage, what surprises did they find, according to the viewpoint?

The United States is facing a huge solid-waste disposal problem, especially in urban areas. US citizens produce more than 4 lbs (~2 kg) of waste per person per day, more waste than can be disposed of in an environmentally sound but economic and local manner. Currently totals represent an increase of more than 60% over 1960 per capita waste generation. Most landfills are within 5 to 10 years of closing unless current facilities are expanded or new landfills opened. Urban areas lack space for new landfills due to the associated urban sprawl of affluent suburbs that uphold a NIMBY, "Not-In-My-Back-Yard," mentality. New England and the rest of the northeast is the most pressed region in the US. Costs to dispose of municipal solid waste have skyrocketed in recent years as well. The evidence indicates that we currently face a national waste crisis, and perhaps our basic premise for solid waste management must change if we are to survive the next decade or two. . . .

Municipalities generate approximately 154 million metric tons of waste each year but they are not the only sources of solid waste in the US. The primary sources of solid waste are split between livestock (39%), extraction and processing ore minerals (38%), crops (14%), municipalities (5%), and industry (3%), totaling over 4 billion tons of solid waste each year. The vast (> 90%) majority is linked to mining and agricultural activities. The mining and agricultural wastes, however, are not pressing problems. Mining wastes are typically dealt with on site and buried in the underground mine, or the open-pit. These pulverized wastes are covered with a layer of soil to prevent the leaching of sulfur and other heavy metals that would have otherwise induced acidification and delivery of toxic compounds to the environment. Agricultural wastes are typically added to local soils where microbes decompose the organic materials and return the organic bound nutrients to the soil.

Serious Environmental Consequences

Even though the quantity of industrial wastes is small in comparison to other major sources, their environmental consequences are high. The ~50 million metric tons of solid industrial wastes each year are categorized by their impact on the environment, by law, into "toxic," "corrosive," "ignitable" or "otherwise hazardous material" categories. The materials are also strongly regulated with "cradle to grave", i.e., manufacture to disposal, federal legislation. It stems from the media coverage and public outcry over the Love Canal problems of the early 1970s [when dangerous industrial pollution was discovered in a New York town]. The US is still swamped with the cleanup of approximately 40,000 known contaminated sites due to unsound pre-1970s indiscriminate dumping of industrial wastes. The cleanup will keep lawyers, environmental engineers, government officials, and many others busy for decades.

FAST FACT

In 2008 a survey of landfills found that 82 percent of surveyed landfill cells had leaks, and 41 percent had leaks larger than one square foot, according to Zero Waste America.

Municipal waste disposal is an environmental problem that costs users billions of dollars each year. The EPA [US Environmental Protection Agency] reported that the typical composition, before recycling, includes paper, yard wastes, food wastes, plastics, metals, rubber, leather & textiles, wood, glass, and other materials including disposable diapers. These numbers exclude construction and demolition debris, biosolids like sewage sludge, industrial wastes and other waste materials that might also be disposed [of] in a landfill. The refuse is not harmless. A wide variety of toxic and other hazardous materials are included in the "other" materials category and sent to landfills every day from the home and the other sources. They include poisons, corrosive cleaning agents, disinfectants, unused prescription drugs, solvents such as paint thinner and dry-cleaning fluids, insecticides and pesticides, heavy metals, and so on. Unfortunately,

Municipal Solid Waste Generation Rates, 1960–2010

In 2010, Americans generated about 250 million tons of trash, or about 4.43 pounds per person per day.

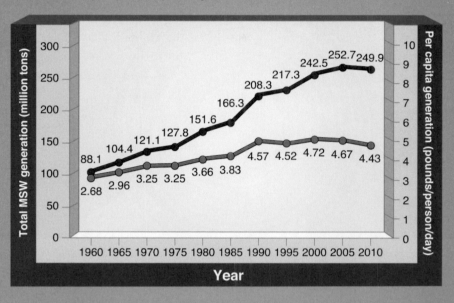

Taken from: EPA, 2012. www.epa.gov/epawaste/nonhaz/municipal/index.htm.

even these small amounts are at sufficiently high concentrations to pollute and degrade nearby air, water and soils.

Sanitary Landfills

Sanitary landfills are designed to "concentrate and contain" our solid waste at a specific site and minimal environmental cost. Each day, a layer of waste is compacted by heavy machinery and buried under a layer of earth or clean construction debris to keep out the vermin, confine the refuse, reduce the odors, and divert leachate-forming rain water from entering the landfill. Once the site is full, the entire landfill is covered by a thick layer of earth, and the land is typically used for other purposes, including parks, pastureland, parking lots, golf courses, and other uses not requiring excavation. Evanston [Illinois] is famous for its Mt. Trashmore, a ski resort built on an abandoned landfill.

Landfills contain many toxic chemicals that leak into the surrounding environment and cause serious pollution.

These uses are only possible if the leakage of noxious gases and/or toxins is minimal. Once a landfill is closed, however, city/county managers face significant hurdles to find more space to dispose [of] the constant stream of solid waste, or ship their trash elsewhere.

Unfortunately, landfills leak gaseous, liquid and solid materials. Bacterial decomposition of organic refuse generates gases, and gas composition changes if the process is aerobic or anaerobic. Initially the organic refuse is decomposed aerobically, producing carbon dioxide (CO_2) and water (H_2O), and perhaps some sulfur dioxide (SO_2) and other gases. Due to the landfill's isolation from the atmosphere, the bacteria quickly consume the available oxygen. Then anaerobic bacteria decompose the remaining organic material and generate gases like methane (CH_4) and the rotten egg smelling hydrogen sulfide (H_2S) if sulfate is available. Typically, the ground cover traps the gases in the landfill, and they must be vented to prevent explosions from the accumulating pressure. In larger facilities, the methane can be collected, stripped of other gases, and used as natural gas. At smaller sites where methane recovery is less economic, the vented gas can be burned onsite.

Bacterial decomposition is very slow. Archaeologists in the southwest have unearthed capped landfills to find readable newsprint and uneaten hot dogs in 40-year-old garbage.

Liquid pollutants, commonly called leachate, can escape from landfills to contaminate surface or ground water. It forms when water percolating through the refuse, collects and dissolves chemicals from the refuse. The water originates as rainfall or groundwater, especially if the protective layer above or below the landfill is permeable. The exact composition of the leachate depends on the water soluble/transportable materials homeowners throw out with the garbage, and may include poisons, corrosive cleaning agents, disinfectants, unused prescription drugs, solvents such as paint thinner and dry-cleaning fluids, insecticides and pesticides, heavy metals, and so on. This list excludes other compounds that may originate from industries or wastewater facilities. Leachate contamination problems were particularly problematic in older sites when landfills typically lacked impermeable barriers beneath the landfill and were typically sited in valleys and other areas near or below the water table. Leakages were also un-noticed early on because the leakage was underground and out of sight. . . .

Alternatives exist to landfills that can alleviate the total tonnage sent to landfills each year. Composting, incineration, and the three R's, recycle, reuse and source reduction, are the primary alternatives to landfills. Each alternative has numerous benefits, and each has numerous environmental problems and socioeconomic pitfalls.

EVALUATING THE AUTHOR'S ARGUMENTS:

The author of the viewpoint you have just read is a scientist, and he uses some scientific language in presenting his arguments. What is the effect of this kind of language? Does the author's use of chemical notation and difficult vocabulary make his argument more effective or less? Why?

Incinerating Garbage Can Produce Much-Needed Clean Energy

"The Environmental Protection Agency . . . applies strict environmental rules to waste-to-energy plants."

US Energy Information Administration

The following viewpoint was created by the US Energy Information Administration (EIA) to explain how waste-to-energy facilities can generate renewable energy from plants and animals. The viewpoint emphasizes the advantages of creating energy this way, contending that a gradual shift to using plants and animals for energy will reduce the nation's reliance on fossil fuels and also reduce greenhouse gas emissions. Although burning garbage to produce energy could be dangerous, the viewpoint argues, the federal government has strict rules that protect the environment and public health. The EIA, part of the US Environmental Protection Agency, collects, analyzes, and distributes independent and impartial energy information.

US Energy Information Administration, *Renewable Biomass*, 2012.

1. Why, according to the viewpoint, is biomass considered a renewable energy source?
2. How much of our typical household trash can be burned, as reported in the viewpoint?
3. According to the viewpoint, what is the major advantage of burning waste?

Biomass is organic material made from plants and animals (microorganisms). Biomass contains stored energy from the sun. Plants absorb the sun's energy in a process called photosynthesis. The chemical energy in plants gets passed on to animals and people that eat them.

Biomass is a renewable energy source because we can always grow more trees and crops, and waste will always exist. Some examples of biomass fuels are wood, crops, manure, and some garbage.

When burned, the chemical energy in biomass is released as heat. If you have a fireplace, the wood you burn in it is a biomass fuel. Wood waste or garbage can be burned to produce steam for making electricity, or to provide heat to industries and homes.

Converting Biomass to Other Forms of Energy

Burning biomass is not the only way to release its energy. Biomass can be converted to other useable forms of energy, such as methane gas or transportation fuels, such as ethanol and biodiesel.

Methane gas is the main ingredient of natural gas. Smelly stuff, like rotting garbage, and agricultural and human waste, release methane gas—also called "landfill gas" or "biogas."

Crops like corn and sugar cane can be fermented to produce ethanol. Biodiesel, another transportation fuel, can be produced from left-over food products like vegetable oils and animal fats.

Biomass fuels provided about 4% of the energy used in the United States in 2011. Of this, about 45% was from wood and wood-derived biomass, 44% from biofuels (mainly ethanol), and about 11% from municipal waste. Researchers are trying to develop ways to burn more biomass and less fossil fuels. Using biomass for energy may cut back on waste and greenhouse gas emissions. . . .

Waste-to-Energy

Garbage, often called municipal solid waste (MSW), is the source of about 6% of the total biomass energy consumed in the United States. MSW contains biomass (or biogenic) materials like paper, cardboard, food scraps, grass clippings, leaves, wood, and leather products, and other non-biomass combustible materials, mainly plastics and other synthetic materials made from petroleum.

Americans produce more and more waste each year. In 1960, the average American threw away 2.7 pounds of trash a day. Today, each American throws away about 4.4 pounds of trash every day. Of that, about 1.5 pounds are recycled or composted. What do we do with the rest? One option is to burn it. (Burning is sometimes called combustion.) About 85% of our household trash is material that will burn, and most of that is biogenic, or material that is made from biomass (plant or animal products). About 62% of MSW (by weight) is biogenic.

Just as corn can be processed into ethanol for fuel, corn cobs, husks, stalks, and other organic garbage can be turned into fuels or burned for energy.

Today, we can burn MSW in special waste-to-energy plants and use its heat energy to make steam to heat buildings or to generate electricity. There are about 87 waste-to-energy plants in the United States that generate electricity or produce steam. In 2010, these plants burned about 12% of MSW and generated 14 million kilowatt hours of electricity, about the same amount used by 1.2 million U.S. households. The biogenic material in MSW contributes about 55% of the energy when MSW is burned in waste-to-energy facilities. Many large landfills also generate electricity with the methane gas that is produced as biomass decomposes in the landfills.

FAST FACT

Through incineration, one ton of garbage generates about 525 kilowatt-hours of electricity, enough energy to heat a typical office building for one day.

Waste-to-Energy Plants Also Dispose of Waste

Providing electricity is not the major advantage of waste-to-energy plants. It actually costs more to generate electricity at a waste-to-energy plant than it does at a coal, nuclear, or hydropower plant.

The major advantage of burning waste is that it reduces the amount of material that we bury in landfills. Waste-to-energy plants burned about 29 million tons of MSW in 2010. Burning MSW reduces the volume of waste by about 87%. . . .

Burning municipal solid waste (MSW, or garbage) and wood waste to produce energy means that less of it has to get buried in landfills. Like plants that burn coal, waste-to-energy plants produce air pollution when the fuel is burned to produce steam or electricity. Burning garbage releases the chemicals and substances found in the waste. Some of these chemicals can be dangerous to people, the environment, or both, if they are not properly controlled.

Incinerators and waste-to-energy power plants must use technology to prevent harmful gases and particles from coming out of their smoke stacks. The Environmental Protection Agency (EPA) applies strict environmental rules to waste-to-energy plants. The EPA requires waste-to-energy plants to use anti-pollution devices, including scrubbers, fabric filters, and electrostatic precipitators to capture air pollutants. . . .

Waste-to-Energy plants are also a growing source of energy in Europe.

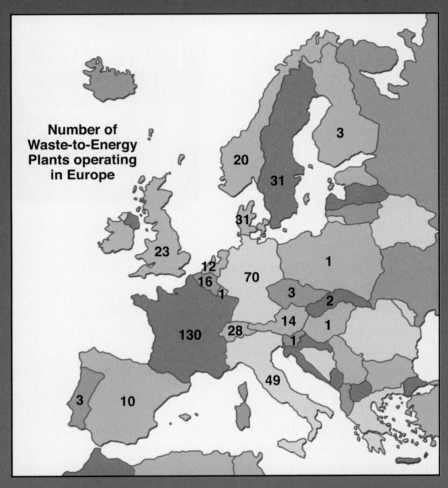

Number of
Waste-to-Energy
Plants operating
in Europe

Taken from: Confederation of European Waste-to-Energy Plants, 2011. www.cewep.eu/media/www.cewep.eu/org/
med_511/767_2011-08-24_map_2009.pdf.

The EPA wants to ensure that harmful gases and particles don't go out the smokestack into the air. Scrubbers clean chemical gas emissions by spraying a liquid into the gas stream to neutralize the acids. Fabric filters and electrostatic precipitators remove particles from the combustion gases. The particles—called fly-ash—are then mixed with the ash that is removed from the bottom of the waste-to-energy plant's furnace.

A waste-to-energy furnace burns at such high temperatures (1,800 to 2,000°F) that many complex chemicals naturally break down into simpler, less harmful compounds. This chemical change is a kind of built-in anti-pollution device.

Disposing of Ash from Waste-to-Energy Plants

Another challenge is the disposal of the ash after combustion. Ash can contain high concentrations of various metals that were present in the original waste. Textile dyes, printing inks, and ceramics, for example, contain the metals lead and cadmium.

Separating waste before combustion can solve part of the problem. Because batteries are the largest source of lead and cadmium in municipal waste, they should not be put into regular trash. Fluorescent light bulbs should also not be put in trash because they contain small amounts of mercury.

The EPA tests ash from waste-to-energy plants to make sure it's not hazardous. The test looks for chemicals and metals that would contaminate ground water by trickling through a landfill. Ash that is considered safe is used in municipal solid waste landfills as a daily or final cover layer, to build roads, to make cement blocks, and even to make artificial reefs for marine animals.

> **EVALUATING THE AUTHOR'S ARGUMENTS:**
>
> Many of the viewpoints you will read in this book use a formal, detached tone to help establish credibility and a sense that the authors are objective. The author of the viewpoint you have just read, on the other hand, uses more inclusive language, referring several times to the waste that "we" generate, or speculating that "you" might burn wood in a fireplace. How does this kind of language affect the way you respond to the viewpoint?

Waste Incineration Produces Pollution and Little Energy

> *"Even the most technologically advanced incinerators release thousands of pollutants that contaminate our air, soil and water."*

Global Alliance for Incinerator Alternatives

The following viewpoint, from the Global Alliance for Incinerator Alternatives (GAIA), argues that waste-to-energy plants are expensive to operate and are dangerous to public health. Although regulations and new technologies help manage emissions from these plants, the viewpoint contends, the plants still generate a great deal of pollution. Because waste-to-energy plants create little energy and few jobs, the viewpoint concludes, it would be wiser to focus on recycling as waste management goes forward. GAIA is a worldwide alliance of groups and individuals in over ninety countries who work against incinerators and for safe, sustainable, and just alternatives. For data references, please see http://www.no-burn.org/incinerators-myths-vs-facts-2/ Incinerator_Myths_vs_Facts%20Feb2012.pdf.

AS YOU READ, CONSIDER THE FOLLOWING QUESTIONS:

1. According to the viewpoint, what kinds of illnesses can be caused by exposure to ultra-fine particles emitted by waste-to-energy plants?
2. As reported in the viewpoint, did a recent study conducted in the United Kingdom show that new incinerators are more efficient or less efficient than older plants?
3. How does the cost of generating electricity in waste-to-energy plants compare with the costs of using coal-fired or nuclear plants, according to the viewpoint?

I ncineration is a waste treatment technology that involves burning commercial, residential and hazardous waste. Incineration converts discarded materials, including paper, plastics, metals and food scraps into bottom ash, fly ash, combustion gases, air pollutants, wastewater, wastewater treatment sludge and heat. There are 113 waste incinerators in the U.S. and 86 of these are used to generate electricity. No new incinerators have been built in the U.S. after 1997, due to public opposition, identified health risks, high costs, and the increase of practices such as recycling and composting. In recent years, the incinerator industry has tried to expand their sector by marketing their facilities as "Waste to Energy" (WTE), using misleading claims.

MYTH 1: Waste Incineration is a source of renewable energy.

FACT: Municipal waste is non-renewable, consisting of discarded materials such as paper, plastic and glass that are derived from finite natural resources such as forests that are being depleted at unsustainable rates. Burning these materials in order to generate electricity creates a demand for "waste" and discourages much-needed efforts to conserve resources, reduce packaging and waste and encourage recycling and composting. More than 90% of materials currently disposed of in incinerators and landfills can be reused, recycled and composted. Providing subsidies or incentives for incineration encourages local governments to destroy these materials, rather than investing in environmentally sound and energy conserving practices such as recycling and composting.

MYTH 2: Modern incinerators have pollution control devices such as filters and scrubbers that make them safe for communities.

FACT: All incinerators pose considerable risk to the health and environment of neighboring communities as well as that of the general population. Even the most technologically advanced incinerators release thousands of pollutants that contaminate our air, soil and water. Many of these pollutants enter the food supply and concentrate up through the food chain. Incinerator workers and people living near incinerators are particularly at high risk of exposure to dioxin and other contaminants. A recent study published in the *American Economic Review* found that among U.S. industries, the waste incineration industry has the highest ratio of negative economic impacts from air pollution compared to the financial value added by the industry.

The New York Department of Conservation found that the state's incinerators emit up to 14 times more mercury as coal-fired power plants per unit of energy. In 2009, New York incinerators emitted a total of 36% more mercury than its coal plants.

In newer incinerators, air pollution control devices such as air filters capture and concentrate some of the pollutants; but they don't eliminate them. The captured pollutants are transferred to other by-products such as fly ash, bottom ash, boiler ash/slag, and wastewater treatment sludge that are then released into the environment. However, even modern pollution control devices such as air filters do not prevent the escape of many hazardous emissions such as ultra-fine particles. Ultra-fine particles are particles produced from burning materials (including PCBs, dioxins and furans), which are smaller in size than what is currently regulated or monitored by the U.S. EPA. These particles can be lethal, causing cancer, heart attacks, strokes, asthma, and pulmonary disease. It is estimated that airborne particulates cause the deaths of over 2 million people worldwide each year. In the U.S. communities of color, low-

FAST FACT

Because of the relatively high carbon dioxide emissions from waste-to-energy plants, the US Environmental Protection Agency has not issued a permit for construction of any new plants since 1990.

Critics say that the incineration of garbage for energy produces more pollution than energy.

income communities, and indigenous communities are exposed to a disproportionate burden of such toxins.

Finally, U.S. regulatory agencies have found that incinerators are prone to various types of malfunctions, system failures and breakdowns, which routinely lead to serious air pollution control problems and increased emissions that are dangerous to public health.

MYTH 3: Modern incinerators produce less carbon dioxide than alternatives.

FACT: Burning waste contributes to climate change. Incinerators emit more carbon dioxide (CO_2) per unit of electricity (2988 lbs/MWh) than coal-fired power plants (2249 lbs/MWh). According to the U.S. EPA, "waste to energy" incinerators and landfills contribute far higher levels of greenhouse gas [GHG] emissions and overall energy throughout their lifecycles than source reduction, reuse and recycling of the same materials. Incineration also drives a climate changing cycle of new resources pulled out of the earth, processed in factories, shipped around the world, and then wasted in incinerators and landfills.

Denmark—the poster child of Europe's incinerator industry—recently discovered that its incinerators were releasing double the quantity of carbon dioxide than originally estimated, and had probably been doing so for years, causing Denmark to miss its Kyoto Protocol GHG reduction targets.

In contrast, a 2009 study by the EPA concluded that up to 42% of U.S. GHG emissions could be impacted through zero waste strategies such as recycling and composting.

MYTH 4: *Modern incinerators efficiently produce electricity.*

FACT: *All incinerators are a massive waste of energy.* Due to the low calorific value of waste, *incinerators are only able to make small amounts of energy* while destroying large amounts of reusable materials. While older incinerators generate electricity at very low efficiency rates of 19–27%, a recent UK study found that conversion efficiencies of new incineration technologies are even lower. Conversely, zero waste practices such as recycling and composting serve to conserve three to five times the amount of energy produced by waste incineration. The amount of energy wasted in the U.S. by not recycling aluminum and steel cans, paper, printed materials, glass, and plastic is equal to the annual output of 15 medium-sized power plants.

MYTH 5: *Incinerators provide jobs for communities.*

FACT: *Recycling creates 10–20 times more jobs than incinerators.* Incinerators require huge capital investment, but they offer relatively few jobs when compared to recycling. With a national recycling rate of less than 33%, the U.S. recycling industries currently provide over 800,000 jobs. *A national recycling rate of 75% would create 1.5 million jobs.*

MYTH 6: *Incinerators are an affordable option.*

FACT: *Incinerators are the most expensive method to generate energy and to handle waste, while also creating significant economic burdens for host cities.* According to the U.S. Energy Information Administration Annual Energy Outlook 2010, the projected capital cost of new waste incinerator facilities is $8,232 per kilowatt hour. That is twice the cost of coal-fired power and 60 percent more than nuclear energy. Waste incinerator operations and maintenance costs are ten times greater than coal and four times greater than nuclear.

Billions of taxpayer dollars are spent subsidizing the construction and operations of incinerators. In 2011, Harrisburg, PA became the largest U.S. city to declare bankruptcy, and the financial blame rests squarely on the shoulders of its staggering debt payments for upgrades

The Waste Disposal Hierarchy

The Waste Disposal Hierarchy helps guide local and national visions and policies for waste management around the world. While simply disposing of waste is the most-used method, it is actually the least desirable.

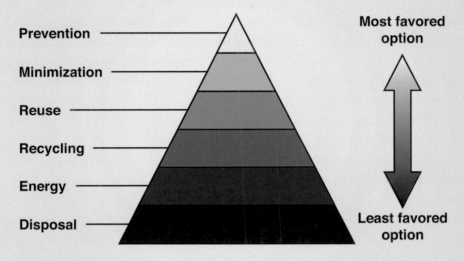

Prevention
Minimization
Reuse
Recycling
Energy
Disposal

Most favored option

Least favored option

Taken from: *Research Trends*, 2010. www.researchtrends.com/issue19-september-2010/research-and-practice-in-waste-management/.

at the city's incinerator. Detroit taxpayers have spent over $1.2 billion dollars in debt service payments from constructing and upgrading the world's largest waste incinerator. As a result, residents have had to pay high trash disposal fees of over $150 per ton. The city could have saved over $55 million in just one year if it had never built the incinerator. For a fraction of these costs, investments in recycling, reuse and remanufacturing would create significantly more business and employment opportunities.

MYTH 7: Incinerators are compatible with recycling.

FACT: Incinerators burn many valuable resources that can be recycled and composted, and incinerators compete for the same materials as recycling programs. Because of the extremely high costs of constructing and operating an incinerator, spending taxpayer money for an incinerator means that there are significantly less funds to invest in more affordable solutions. More than two thirds of the materials we use are still burned or buried, despite the fact that we can cost-effectively recycle the vast majority of what we waste.

MYTH 8: Countries like Denmark that are expanding incineration have the highest recycling rates and they only burn materials that cannot be recycled.

FACT: Countries and regions in Europe that have high waste incineration rates typically recycle less. Data for household waste from Denmark in 2005 clearly shows that regions with expanded incineration have lower recycling and regions with lower incineration do more recycling. It's worth noting that Denmark's recycling rate is well behind other regions of Europe such as Flanders in Belgium, which recycles 71% of municipal waste.

According to Eurostat in 2007, Denmark generates some of the highest per capita waste in the EU [European Union] (over 1762 lbs. each year) and over 80% of what is burned in Danish incinerators is recyclable and compostable. A 2009 study reported that Europe throws away resources worth over $6 billion dollars every year by burning and burying materials that can be recycled.

MYTH 9: Modern European incinerators produce clean energy, less pollution.

FACT: Waste incinerators in the EU continue to pollute the climate and cause significant public health risk, while burning billions of dollars-worth of valuable, non-renewable resources. A recent public health impacts report states that modern incinerators in the EU are a major source of ultra-fine particulate emissions. In 2009, the Advertising Standards Agency in the UK banned the SITA Cornwall waste company from distributing its booklet on incineration for, among other things, making unsubstantiated claims that the UK Health Protection Agency stated that modern incinerators are safe.

MYTH 10: The EU is way ahead, and the U.S. lags behind in waste reduction.

FACT: U.S. communities have been pioneers in the field of Zero Waste, as have many communities in Europe that prioritize zero waste above incineration, while many EU countries are ahead of the U.S. in terms of national programs such as healthcare and climate change mitigation. Zero Waste is *the design and management of products and processes to reduce the volume and toxicity of waste and materials, conserve and recover all resources, and not burn or bury them.* Americans can be proud of some of the benchmarks we have achieved in reducing waste through Zero Waste strategies:

- The Commonwealth of Massachusetts and the States of Rhode Island, Delaware and California have either banned or seriously restricted new waste incinerators, in favor of Zero Waste practices and policies.
- Massachusetts, California, Wisconsin and Washington prioritize Zero Waste practices and policies.
- The U.S. has led the world in the implementation of curbside recycling programs, with more communities (40+) committed to Zero Waste goals than all of Europe, including the cities of Oakland (CA), Los Angeles (CA), Seattle (WA) and Austin (TX).
- The city of San Francisco has achieved a 75% recycling rate of all municipal and commercial waste, aims to get to Zero Waste by the year 2020, and has created over 1000 local jobs in the sector.

EVALUATING THE AUTHOR'S ARGUMENTS:

The two viewpoints you have just read are at times in direct disagreement. For example, the viewpoint from the EIA states that biomass is renewable, in part because "we can always grow more trees, and waste will always exist"; GAIA states that waste is nonrenewable, and that forests "are being depleted at unsustainable rates." The two also disagree about whether the federal government is able to control pollution from waste-to-energy plants. How can readers weigh the validity of such contradictory claims? Look carefully at the language of each claim. Can both viewpoints be right? Explain.

Chapter 2

Is Recycling Effective?

Recycling is controversial because although it reuses materials, the process causes pollution of its own that may offset the benefits.

Viewpoint 1

Recycling Is a Waste of Time and Energy

Daniel K. Benjamin

"[Mandatory recycling] programs force people to squander valuable resources in a quixotic quest to save what they would sensibly discard."

In the following viewpoint economist Daniel K. Benjamin challenges some common beliefs about the benefits of recycling. Rather than blaming packaging for increasing the amount of trash we generate, he argues, we should acknowledge that packaging leads to less wasted by-products, food spoilage, and disease. Rather than simply assuming that recycling is better for the environment, he argues, we should consider the extra pollution caused by the trucks that transport materials to be recycled. The failure to look carefully at all the costs of recycling, he concludes, leads to waste. Benjamin is a senior fellow at the Property and Environment Research Center, a think tank dedicated to improving environmental quality through property rights and free markets.

Recycling has always been an integral part of dealing with waste products in the United States, as in much of the world. But until recently, decisions about whether to recycle or not were generally left to individuals and firms.

About 25 years ago, Americans' view of trash changed swiftly and radically. Trash vaulted from the local to the state and national level. State legislatures debated alternative means of disposal, the Environmental Protection Agency [EPA] made rubbish a matter of federal regulation, and Congress and the Supreme Court found themselves in the midst of contentious debates over interstate garbage trucks and barges.

Aroused by fear of a garbage crisis and spurred by the misleading story of the garbage barge *Mobro* [a barge that in 1987 traveled for six months looking for a place to dump its load of trash], Americans lost their sense of perspective on rubbish. A new consensus emerged: Reduce, reuse, and—especially—recycle became the only ecologically responsible solutions to America's perceived crisis. Public rhetoric was increasingly dominated by claims that were dubious or patently false. . . .

Myth: Packaging Is Our Problem

Packaging is ubiquitous in the marketplace and in the landfill. Indeed, it amounts to about 30 percent of what goes into landfills, down from 36 percent in 1970. Many people argue that the easiest way to save landfill space is to reduce the amount of packaging Americans use, and they urge that packaging reduction should be mandatory if manufacturers will not cut back of their own volition. The arithmetic seems simple: one pound less of packaging means one pound less in landfills. But as with many facts of rubbish, less is sometimes more, in this case in more ways than one.

Packaging can *reduce* total rubbish produced and total resources used. The average household in the United States generates less trash each year—fully one-third less—than does the average household in Mexico. The reason is that our intensive use of packaging yields less waste and breakage and, on balance, less total rubbish. For example, for every 1,000 chickens brought to market using modern processing

In 1987, the garbage crisis was brought to the public's attention when the garbage barge Mobro *searched for over six months for a disposal site.*

and packaging, approximately 17 pounds of packaging are used (and thus disposed of). But at least 2,000 pounds of waste by-products are recycled into marketable products (such as pet food) because the processing takes place in a commercial facility rather than in the home. Most of these by-products would end up in landfills if packaging did not make commercial processing feasible.

Quite apart from reducing landfill and wastewater loads, packaging saves resources by reducing breakage. The resulting higher wealth enables us to do things we otherwise could not do, ranging from educating doctors to keeping ecologically valuable land out of agricultural or commercial usage. Because sanitary packaging reduces food spoilage, it also reduces the incidence of food poisoning. And there is also the matter of mere convenience. Imagine shopping for milk, peanut butter, or toothpaste if such goods were not prepackaged. . . .

Myth: Recycling Always Protects the Environment

To many people, it is axiomatic that recycling protects the environment. The position of the Natural Resources Defense Council is typical: "It is virtually beyond dispute that manufacturing products from recyclables instead of from virgin raw materials—making, for instance, paper out of old newspapers instead of virgin timber—causes less pollution and imposes fewer burdens on the earth's natural habitat and biodiversity." Yet this assertion is not beyond dispute; it is wrong in many instances.

Recycling is a manufacturing process, and therefore it too has an environmental impact. The U.S. Office of Technology Assessment (OTA) says that it is "usually not clear whether secondary manufacturing [such as recycling] produces less pollution per ton of material processed than primary manufacturing processes." Indeed, the Office of Technology Assessment goes on

> **FAST FACT**
>
> More than seven thousand American communities, as well as many European countries, have pay-as-you-go systems, which charge customers a certain amount for every bag of trash they throw out but do not specify whether recyclables may be in the bags. These systems encourage consumers to recycle without requiring them to.

"I worry that the warm glow from your sense of smug self-satisfaction could be harming the environment."

to explain why: Recycling changes the nature of pollution, sometimes increasing it and sometimes decreasing it.

For example, the EPA and various private researchers have compared the environmental impacts of virgin paper processing with those of recycled paper processing. While recycling is less polluting than virgin processing on many dimensions, in some cases the adverse environmental impacts of recycled processing are more severe. Which combination of pollutants is preferable remains unknown. Similar mixed results have been found for steel and aluminum production. Indeed, over the past 25 years, a large body of literature devoted to life-cycle analyses of products from their birth to death has repeatedly found that recycling can increase pollution as well as decrease it.

This effect is particularly apparent in the case of curbside recycling, which is mandated or strongly encouraged by governments in many communities. Curbside recycling requires that more trucks be used to collect the same amount of waste materials, trucks that pick up perhaps four to eight pounds of recyclables, rather than forty or more pounds of rubbish. Los Angeles estimated that because it instituted curbside recycling, its fleet of trucks is twice as large as it otherwise would have been—800 versus 400 trucks. This means more iron ore and coal mining, more steel and rubber manufacturing, more petroleum extracted and refined for fuel—and, of course, all that extra air pollution in the Los Angeles basin as the 400 added trucks cruise the streets.

Misinformation Leads to Waste

Recycling is a long-practiced, productive, indeed essential, element of the market system. Informed, *voluntary* recycling conserves resources and raises our wealth, enabling us to achieve valued ends that would otherwise be impossible. In sharp contrast, however, *mandatory* recycling programs, in which people are compelled to do what they will not do voluntarily, routinely make society worse off. Such programs force people to squander valuable resources in a quixotic quest to save what they would sensibly discard. On balance, mandatory recycling programs lower our wealth.

Misinformation about the costs and benefits of recycling is as destructive as mandatory recycling programs, for it induces people to engage in wasteful activity. Public service campaigns and "educational" programs that exaggerate the benefits of recycling fall into this category, but there are other offenders as well. For example, bottle and can deposit laws, which effectively misinform people about the true value of used beverage containers, induce people to waste resources collecting and processing items that appear to be worth five (or even ten) cents, given their redemption prices, but in fact are worth a penny or less to society. Similarly, costly government-run recycling programs that pick up recyclables at no charge give people the incentive to engage in too much recycling. They give the appearance that the programs are without cost, when in fact they consume valuable resources that could be used in far more highly valued pursuits.

The free market system is eminently capable of providing both disposal and recycling in an amount and mix that creates the greatest wealth for society. This makes possible the widest and most satisfying range of human endeavors. Simply put, market prices are sufficient to induce the trashman to come, and to make his burden bearable, and neither he nor we can hope for any better than that.

EVALUATING THE AUTHOR'S ARGUMENTS:

In the viewpoint you have just read, the author devotes three paragraphs to explaining that recycling, as a manufacturing process, generates pollution, "sometimes increasing it and sometimes decreasing it." He reports that recycling is less polluting "in many dimensions," but more polluting "in some cases." How does his lack of specific examples, details and statistics in these paragraphs affect your reading of the viewpoint? It is likely that many of the author's readers would not understand highly technical information if he had given it. In such cases is an author right to strike a confident and authoritative tone and leave out the technical jargon? Explain.

Recycling Is an Important Part of Waste Disposal

"The amount of energy saved differs by material, but almost all recycling processes achieve significant energy savings compared to virgin material production."

US Environmental Protection Agency

In the following viewpoint, the United States Environmental Protection Agency (EPA) reports the benefits of recycling materials. The agency argues that recycling can supply companies with needed raw materials, help create jobs, and be more cost effective than trash collection. The EPA also believes recycling would put less pressure on landfills. The EPA is a United States government agency that was created to protect human health and the environment.

AS YOU READ, CONSIDER THE FOLLOWING QUESTIONS:
1. According to the viewpoint, what are a few of the listed benefits of recycling?
2. As stated in the article, what was the estimated tax revenues generated by the recycling industry in 2001?
3. In 1996, how much money did Ann Arbor, Michigan, spend on recycling and composting?

US Environmental Protection Agency, "Communicating the Benefits of Recycling," EPA.gov, July 27, 2012.

There are significant environmental and economic benefits associated with recycling. Recycling helps create jobs, can be more cost effective than trash collection, reduces the need for new landfills, saves energy, supplies valuable raw materials to industry, and adds significantly to the U.S. economy.

- More Jobs, Economic Development, and Tax Revenue
- More Energy Security
- Less Greenhouse Gas Emissions
- Less Pressure on Landfills and More Natural Resources for Future Generations
- State Economic Impacts

More Jobs, Economic Development, and Tax Revenue

- Recycling creates new businesses that haul, process, and broker recovered materials, as well as companies that manufacture and distribute products made with these recycled materials.
- The recycling and reuse industry consists of approximately 56,000 establishments that employ over 1.1 million people, generate an annual payroll of nearly $37 billion, and gross over $236 billion in annual revenues.
- Unlike the waste management industry, recycling adds value to materials, contributing to a growing labor force including materials sorters, dispatchers, truck drivers, brokers, sales representatives, process engineers, and chemists. These jobs also generally pay above the average national wage, and many are in inner city urban areas where job creation is vital.
- The recycling and reuse industry generates billions in federal, state, and local tax revenues (estimated at $12.9 billion in 2001).

> **FAST FACT**
>
> According to the Aluminum Association, the money generated by recycling aluminum cans more than pays for the cost of collecting them. The revenue from recycling cans helps cover the costs of collecting other, less valuable recyclables.

More Energy Security

- The amount of energy saved differs by material, but almost all recycling processes achieve significant energy savings compared to virgin material production. For example, recycling of aluminum cans saves 95 percent of the energy required to make the same amount of aluminum from virgin sources. For each can recycled, this is enough energy to run a television or computer for three hours.
- By conservative estimates, recycling was projected to save 605 trillion British Thermal Units (BTUs) in 2005, equal to the energy used in 6 million households annually.
- About 4 percent of the U.S.'s total energy consumption is used in the production of all plastic products, and some of this energy can be recovered through the recycling of plastics products after their useful life is ended.
- For each pound of aluminum recovered, Americans save the energy resources to generate about 7.5 kilowatt-hours of electricity. This is enough energy to meet the electric needs of a city the size of Pittsburgh for six years.
- Using glass cullet (e.g., broken glass) allows the glass container industry to reduce energy input to its furnaces. Energy costs drop 2 to 3 percent for every 10 percent cullet used in the manufacturing process.

Less Greenhouse Gas Emissions

- Current evidence suggests that it is likely that human activities have contributed to accelerated warming of the Earth's surface through the increase of emissions of greenhouse gases (GHGs) which have altered the chemical composition of the atmosphere.
- While there is uncertainty regarding the human and ecological impacts of climate change, scientists have identified that our health, agriculture, water resources, forests, wildlife and coastal areas are vulnerable to the changes that global warming may bring.
- In 2005, recycling was projected to avoid—through a combination of energy savings, forest carbon sequestration, and lower methane emissions—48 million metric tons of carbon emissions (MTCE), which is a standard measure of GHG emissions. This is the equivalent of taking 36 million cars off the road for one year.

Recycling cans and bottles uses far less energy than making new objects from raw materials, proponents argue.

Less Pressure on Landfills and More Natural Resources for Future Generations

- Recycling revenues can help defray recycling costs and forestall the need for new disposal capacity as every cubic yard of material recycled is one less cubic yard of landfill space that is required. These avoided costs are part of the "revenues" that recycling brings to a community. For example, in 1996, Ann Arbor, Michigan, spent $71 per ton on recycling and composting, compared to $86 per ton for trash collection and disposal.

- In 1996, 130 million cubic yards of material were diverted from landfills due to recycling and composting. If this amount of material had not been recycled, the U.S. would have needed 64 additional landfills, each with enough capacity to serve the combined city populations of Dallas and Detroit.
- By substituting recovered scrap materials for the use of trees, metal ores, minerals, oil, and other virgin materials, recycling reduces the pressure to expand forestry and mining production, which can be environmentally damaging. For example, recycling one ton of paper saves the equivalent of 17 trees and 7,000 gallons of water.
- Fossil fuels and metals are nonrenewable resources—they cannot be replenished by nature within our lifetimes and are therefore, in limited supply. The more of these materials we extract, the less that remains for future generations.

State Economic Impacts

In addition to the environmental and economic benefits described above, recycling contributes significantly to the economies of states across the U.S., as evidenced below.

- In March 2005, North Carolina issued a study, Recycling Means Business, on the impact of recycling on North Carolina's economy. The study provides a snapshot of the many faces of North Carolina's recycling industry, featuring 42 recycling companies in the state.
- Employment Trends in North Carolina's Recycling Industry quantifies the impact of recycling on jobs in North Carolina.
- The South Carolina Recycling Market Development Advisory Council released a study in 2006, The Economic Impact of the Recycling Industry in South Carolina, indicating that the recycling industry creates an estimated $6.5 billion total economic impact in the state's economy.
- The state of Florida hosts nearly 3,700 recycling and reuse establishments, employing approximately 32,000 people, generating an annual payroll of $765 million and netting $4.4 billion in annual revenues.

- Recycling nets the following economic benefits in the state of Pennsylvania in 2009:
  - Recycling and Reuse Establishments: 3,803
  - Recycling and Reuse Employment: 52,316 jobs
  - Annual Sales Receipts: $20.6 billion
  - Annual Payroll: $2.2 billion

EVALUATING THE AUTHOR'S ARGUMENTS:

The author of the viewpoint you have read provides an absolute and concrete view that recycling benefits society. Would a more objective and less resolute view of recycling affect your opinion and reading of the article? Explain.

Single-Stream Recycling Yields Less-Useful Recycled Materials

Clarissa Morawski

"In general, the final commodities from single stream programs will be more contaminated."

In the following viewpoint Clarissa Morawski compares single-stream recycling programs to other recycling programs and finds that they are not worth their additional costs. One important purpose of recycling, she points out, is to generate materials that can be remade into new products; however, single-stream programs yield less material that can be used this way. Another purpose is to keep garbage out of landfills, she argues, but single-stream programs send more material to landfills than competing programs do. She concludes that single-stream programs cost more to operate and that the additional costs are not justifiable. Morawski is a business consultant with expertise in beverage container recovery systems.

1. What is meant by the term *closed loop* as it is used in the second paragraph of the viewpoint?
2. Which of the three recycling systems compared in the viewpoint—single-stream, dual-stream, and bottle-deposit systems—yields the highest percentage of high-quality recyclable glass?
3. According to the author, why does single-stream recycling appear to cost municipalities more than other systems, even though the costs of collecting the recyclables are less?

This report describes the evolution of single-stream recycling in the United States, the recent downturn in the scrap market for all recyclable materials, and explains factors affecting collection costs. The real purpose of the study, however, is to examine the impacts of single-stream recycling, as compared to other methods, on every step of the recycling process, including:

- Initial ease of collection and collection costs;
- Contamination rates and overall material yield at Material Recovery Facilities (MRFs);
- Impacts on material yield at paper mills;
- Impacts on yield at plastics processors;
- Impacts on paper mills, on quality, quantity, equipment maintenance and costs;
- Impacts on aluminum processors on contamination levels, resulting equipment shutdowns, and profit losses;
- Impacts on glass, including color mixing, suitability for certain end-uses, and increased operating costs; and,
- Impacts on plastic quality and costs.

Recycling's real purpose is to substitute virgin inputs with secondary feedstock at the manufacturing stage. Most lay people, and perhaps most local officials, assume that all recycled items go to their best use. They are shocked to learn that the materials they dutifully put in a recycling bin may in fact wind up in a landfill. The key to achieving the environmental and economic benefits of recycling is to keep the material circulating for as many product lives as possible. This is the closed loop that reduces the need for virgin materials, thus avoiding

Workers at a single-stream recycling plant separate paper, cardboard, and plastic. Critics say that single-stream recycling uses only 60 percent of the waste materials while 40 percent still ends up in landfills.

the energy consumption and greenhouse gas emissions associated with primary materials extraction, transportation and processing.

Ensuring that secondary recovered recyclables are utilized for the highest possible end-use is a critical part of successful diversion. For plastic, high-end uses can have ten to twenty times the environmental benefit in terms of the replacement of virgin materials and those avoided upstream impacts. Using glass to make containers saves much more energy than using recycled glass for other purposes.

Focus: Keep Materials Out of Landfills

The historical focus of residential recycling (in the 1990s) has been on keeping materials out of landfills. This led to creating systems that could collect the greatest volume of material, with less of a focus on final end-use of the materials. Now, in 2009, we see a developing shift in public solid waste policy to focus more on reducing energy use, creation of greenhouse gases, and production of toxics.

In an effort to increase recycling volumes and reduce high recycling collection costs, the waste management sector created single stream recycling collection, which increases efficiencies by collecting more material with less labor and less distance traveled. Automated single stream collection can reduce the number of employees, improve route efficiency, and reduce workers compensation costs. Single stream can encourage residents to place more material in their recycling bin by giving them a larger bin and by simplifying the system.

Broken and Contaminated Materials

Glass is the material most affected by the amount of breakage in each type of collection system. In single-stream programs, it is virtually impossible to prevent glass from breaking as it goes to the curb, is dumped in the truck, gets compacted, gets dumped on the tipping floor of the MRF, is repeatedly driven over by forklifts, and is dumped on conveyor belts to be processed by the MRF. On average, 40% of glass from single-stream collection winds up in landfills, while 20% is small broken glass ("glass fines") used for low-end applications. Only 40% is recycled into containers and fiberglass. About one third of the non-recyclable glass is broken glass, too small to separate for recycling, some of which can be used for sandblasting base, aggregate material, or Alternative Daily Cover (ADC) [used to cover waste in a landfill at the end of each day]. These "down-cycled" uses do not have the same savings in terms of energy conservation and avoided emissions. In contrast, dual-stream systems have an average yield of 90%, and container-deposit systems yield 98% glass available for use in bottle-making. (Only glass that is sorted by color can be used to make glass containers.)

> **FAST FACT**
>
> The Container Recycling Institute estimates that about 2 percent of the sorted material delivered to recycling collection centers is contaminated and must be discarded; for single-stream collection programs, the rate of contamination is 25 percent.

In general, the final commodities from single stream programs will be more contaminated than those that are collected in a dual-stream system or sorted at the curb. This contamination increase often results

Contamination Hurts Paper Recyclers

SP Recycling Corp., a supplier of recycled fiber for news print manufacturers, reports that for every ton of recycled paper the company gets from single-stream processors, 80 percent must be thrown away because it is contaminated with bits of glass and metal.

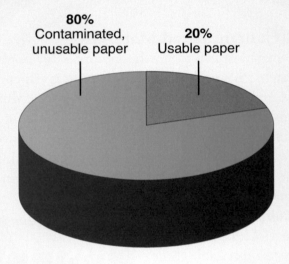

80%
Contaminated,
unusable paper

20%
Usable paper

Taken from: Jim Johnson. "Contamination Is Paper Recyclers' Bane." *Waste & Recycling News*, May 30, 2011.
http://go.galegroup.com/ps/i.do?id=GALE%7CA257881176&v=2.1&u=itsbtrial&it=r&p=GPS&sw=w.

in the commodity being worth less than cleaner material, and can create problems at paper mills, leading to equipment failure, lost productivity and expensive repairs. In other words, the cost savings for a municipality from single-stream collection show up as cost increases for the processors and recyclers. The contaminants are thrown away by the paper mills. So, an item such as a plastic bottle that was recyclable when it was placed at the curb becomes trash by the time it is sorted out as a contaminant by the paper mill.

More Material, Higher Cost

A study conducted in 2002 by Eureka Recycling (of St. Paul, Minnesota) compared five different collection methods, and found that single-stream collected 21% more material than the baseline method. However, the study did not ultimately recommend a single-stream system, because the lower collection costs were outweighed by higher processing costs and lower material revenues.

In another study, Daniel Lantz of Ontario, Canada–based Metro Waste Paper Recovery analyzed recovery rates for three single-stream and four dual-stream programs in that province. The study found that a drop in collection costs sees a commensurate rise in processing costs. In an article for *Resource Recycling* magazine, Mr. Lantz concludes that the supposed benefits of single-stream systems over dual-stream do not outweigh their costs:

> In summary, with increased processing costs and lost revenues in total far exceeding collection savings in most instances (and zero under alternating-week collection), overall single-stream recycling does not show the cost advantage that was originally anticipated. As well, the expected increases in capture rate are also not apparent. Overall, dual-stream recycling still appears to be more advantageous.

In spite of these challenging conditions and their impact on the current demand for recyclables, recycling continues to be a vital component of a national strategy to conserve resources, supply the manufacturing base and reduce greenhouse gas emissions, toxics and waste going to landfills and incinerators.

EVALUATING THE AUTHOR'S ARGUMENTS:

The focus in the viewpoint you have just read is on very practical matters: the amount of material that can be collected and recycled and the financial costs of doing so. Although the author briefly mentions issues that could be more dramatic (creation of greenhouse gases, labor, workers compensation costs), she does not linger on these issues or use any emotional language in her argument. How are this approach and language likely to resonate with different kinds of readers? What can you infer about the author's target audience from her use of writing strategies?

Get the Word Out: It's Time to Mingle; When Cities Switch to Single-Stream, Education Is Crucial

"Supporters of commingled systems say the one-bin system leads to greater participation and greater volumes of recycling."

Amanda Smith-Teutsch

In the following viewpoint journalist Amanda Smith-Teutsch outlines the benefits of single-stream recycling. Residents no longer have to sort recyclables into different containers, she explains, making it more likely that they will participate in recycling. It is important, she contends, for communities to educate their citizens about how a new recycling plan will work—especially in terms of what can and cannot be collected. Communities that make the switch and spend time and money on education, she concludes, will see an increase in the

Amanda Smith-Teutsch, "Get the Word Out: It's Time to Mingle," *Waste & Recycling News,* vol. 16, no. 23, March 21, 2011, p. 1. Copyright © 2011 by Waste & Recycling News. All rights reserved. Reproduced by permission.

amount of material collected for recycling and a decrease in the cost of collecting. Smith-Teutsch, a former reporter for *Waste & Recycling News*, writes a blog about recycling called *eScrap Beat*.

AS YOU READ, CONSIDER THE FOLLOWING QUESTIONS:
1. What problems did Iowa residents have with their old eighteen-gallon recycling totes, as described in the viewpoint?
2. How much per household did Iowa's Metro Waste Authority spend to educate people about the change to single-stream recycling, as reported in the viewpoint?
3. In Corpus Christi, Texas, what happened to the frequency of garbage collection at the same time that the city began single-stream recycling?

Many cities, looking for decreased costs or increased participation, are abandoning their source-separated recycling programs in favor of commingled curbside collection.

Proponents of separated recycling programs—where residents separate plastics, glass, paper and other recyclables—say the program leads to cleaner commodities and more marketable material.

For example, a 2009 survey by the Container Recycling Institute found significant downstream disadvantages to commingled recycling, from contamination to glass breakage.

Supporters of commingled systems say the one-bin system leads to greater participation and greater volumes of recycling.

Some communities are moving away from the sorted recycling in favor of cheaper single-stream programs that are more likely to see greater participation and greater commodities recovered.

"We had a very successful five-sort program, but it just wasn't doing the job we had hoped for. We were seeing recycling volume increasing, but over the last five years it was in smaller and smaller increments," said Reo Menning, public affairs director for Iowa's Metro Waste Authority.

The MWA handles refuse, recycling and program education for 76,000 households in Iowa. The authority allowed two 18-gallon totes per resident until 2009, and many residents complained about the system—two bins weren't enough, they tended to blow around during wind spells, and people didn't like to sort out their recyclables.

"We had a lot of complaints about sorting," Menning said. "People didn't like to sort, it was a pain. So we had some people who didn't participate—but we still had 80% participation."

So when the authority's collection and processing contracts expired, the MWA put out a request for a proposal for single-stream programs instead of the sorted program in place for 15 years, moving from 18-gallon totes to 96-gallon bins.

"It was a three-year process for us," Menning said. "We toured single-stream facilities, making sure technology was at a place where you could sort single-stream and have quality, marketable material. That was important to us, quality material.

"We spent a great deal of time educating elected officials at each community showing things would get recycled," she said. "There was a lot of skepticism around if you put it all in one cart, will it really get recycled? People were well informed on how the recycling process worked. They know you can't sell it as one big bundle without devaluing the material."

After getting officials to buy into the program, it was time to educate the public on the change. The MWA doubled its educational outreach spending, increasing from $1.14 per household to $2.40 per household. They sent out fliers, community newsletters and reminders, and they got the local media on board. Each area was told exactly how the change would impact individual residents, down to when the cart would be collected and how to load it up.

"We had such low call volume from the rollout, it was pretty miraculous how well it went," Menning said. "It was getting elected officials [to] buy in early on, and doing direct and frequent communication with residents. It was offering two cart sizes and the fact that we had years of education already in place about recycling. We had 4% contamination with single-stream, and we still have that today. We doubled our education outreach during that period of time. That's what worked for us."

Collection costs went down, Menning said. "We're still paying less than we were paying under the five-sort program for collection costs," she said. "The first year we saved $300,000 in collection costs and reduced by 49 cents per household per month in the first year. We pay $2,261,000 a year in collection costs. Saving 40 cents per household, that helps a lot."

In Corpus Christi, Texas, city planners were looking for ways to reduce collection costs for the city's 300,000 residents and increase recycling rates. Every resident in the city had twice-weekly collection for refuse, and as a whole only 16% of the residential waste was being recycled, said Kim Womack, director of public information.

"The response has been absolutely incredible," Womack said. "Prior to single-stream curbside recycling, we were at about 16% recycling rate. For our first load, we were at a 500% increase. We have had an incredible response from our residents."

The change wasn't easy, said Lawrence Mikolajczyk, director of Corpus Christi Solid Waste Services. Mikolajczyk said the reduced

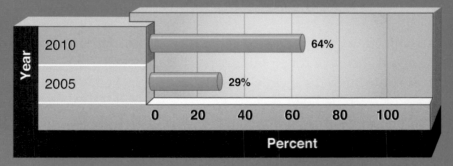

The Growth of Single Stream Recycling

Of people with access to recycling in the United States, the number who have access to single-stream programs has more than doubled since 2005.

Year

2010 — 64%

2005 — 29%

Percent

0   20   40   60   80   100

Taken from: American Forest and Paper Association, 2011. http:www.paperrecycles.org/new/exec_summ_2010.html.

Proponents of single-stream recycling argue that it can lead to greater numbers of people who recycle.

waste collections and increased recycling was proposed as a way to rein in costs during a tough budget year.

"It was during budget time—we'd always attached it to reducing garbage collections from twice a week to once a week so we could realize the most savings," Mikolajczyk said. "That's always a political hotball issue. But because of budget issues, during the last budget process they started looking at it. At one point, they threatened to stop recycling completely."

Then, at the last meeting for the budget on July 15, 2010, the city government approved the recycling plan to move forward, starting Jan. 31, 2011. That gave the city six months to contract with a recycling provider, who may have to upgrade a recycling facility from sorted to single-stream capable; six months to bid out 83,000 recycling carts for residents; and six months to educate everyone about the change in recycling and trash collection frequency.

"Remarkably, when we converted all the garbage routes from twice to once and refactored times on the streets, we were very accurate," Mikolajczyk said. "On the recycling side, we underestimated our residents. We're rocking on right now 95% participation rates out of 83,157 bins. We built some of these routes rather large, because in talking to other municipalities throughout the state, we should expect 50% participation rate."

Public education was key, Womack said.

"Our news media embraced it and helped us every step of the way," she said. "We had inserts in utility bills, and Recyclebank, who is a partner, followed up with a postcard. Something came out every week until the launch—everything from the first carts are arriving in town to the first carts are delivered to refrigerator cards for every resident, showing what could go in cart and what couldn't."

There were about 600 complaints, but participation has skyrocketed.

"Over the first two collection cycles—four weeks—we captured some pretty good numbers. We collected a third of the volume we would have collected in a year in the curbsort system we just replaced," Mikolajczyk said. "We collected 1,080 tons in the first four weeks—and annually had collected 3,000 tons of recyclables."

Costs are also down, he said.

"Our collection budget was $6.3 million before the recycle program; the recycle budget was $1,087 million," Mikolajczyk said. "For the full year, we are hoping to save $2 million from that. This was designed to be budget-neutral, and we have achieved that."

EVALUATING THE AUTHOR'S ARGUMENTS:

In the viewpoint you have just read, the author makes a case in favor of single-stream recycling on the strength of two examples. She does not give national or global figures, but instead focuses on two particular places and shows with precision their changing costs and their changing rates of participation. How does this approach affect your reading of the viewpoint? How willing are you to accept the implication that these two examples can be taken as typical? Why?

Electronics Recycling Makes Sense

Robin Ingenthron

"Even the worst forms of recycling produce less pollution than the cleanest form of mining."

In the following viewpoint Robin Ingenthron takes up some of the common beliefs about the dangers of recycling electronic waste and argues that they are largely exaggerated. The growth in the amount of electronic equipment being discarded is only temporary, he claims, because cell phones and other devices continue to get smaller, and soon all of the older, larger models will be out of circulation. Much of the common wisdom about dangerous heavy metals in electronic waste is also out-of-date, he contends, because newer models of televisions and computer monitors use less hazardous material. Ingenthron operates an electronics recycling company in Vermont.

AS YOU READ, CONSIDER THE FOLLOWING QUESTIONS:

1. What is the meaning of the "lawnmower effect," as explained in the viewpoint?
2. Why, according to the viewpoint, is the lead contained in a cathode ray tube not a serious hazard?
3. Which endangered animal is threatened by the mining of the metal coltan, according to the viewpoint?

Myth: "There Is a Growing Tsunami of E-waste."

The Pitch: Electronics are more disposable, with shorter useful lives. And there is evidence that obsolete electronics are the fastest growing segment of the MSW [municipal solid waste] stream. And the changes in analog TV broadcasts did make old "rabbit ears" TVs obsolete for receiving live broadcasts, unless they are connected to cable or satellite. The pile is just getting bigger and bigger.

These facts are true, but they do not describe production of electronics. The units themselves are getting smaller. There is more computing power in a cell phone today than in a living-room-sized computer at NASA in the 1970s. The increasing tonnage includes "legacy" equipment. A lot of the product being collected at events (think CRT [cathode ray tube] televisions) is coming out after decades of storage. The more recently a state began collecting used electronics, the higher the pounds of "e-waste" per capita. So, there actually has been a wave, but the wave has already crested in places like Massachusetts and California, as the old "old growth" TVs have been cleared out. The tonnage is only "growing" where the collections just recently started. This is the "lawnmower effect"—the longer you wait to mow the lawn, the heavier the bag of clippings. In more mature programs, most of the mass is still older units, but most of the count is from younger units. The wood console TVs which showed Super Bowl X, and the 80 pound Kaypro "laptops", are finite. What we see is not more and more "e-waste" generation, but more "e-waste" collections in more places. . . .

Myth: Electronics Are Dangerously Toxic.

The Pitch: Five pounds of lead in an average CRT. Cadmium phosphors found in piles of CRT glass. As described in King/McCarthy's 2009 publication *Environmental Sociology*, "E-waste today contains a witches' brew of toxic substances such as lead and cadmium in circuit boards; lead oxide and cadmium in monitor cathode ray tubes...." HowStuffWorks, Wikipedia, and many other reputable sources have beaten the drum about toxics in TVs and computers.

It's safe to say that the TV is in its most dangerous state when it's turned on in your living room (varying with the program you are watching). The presence of toxics in computers and monitors, as compared with toxics in automobiles and white goods [major appliances], has been exaggerated. Virtually no computer monitors have cadmium, and there is no liquid mercury in a TV or computer. The lead in CRTs is "vitrified" (chemically bound up, solidified in the glass), the same as in leaded glass crystal dinnerware. CRTs of 40 and 50 years ago used cadmium for yellows or greens, but manufacturers got rid of cadmium by 1970.

What about the poisoned waters in Guiyu, China? First, the poisons emitted from primitive circuit board recycling don't actually come from the circuit boards, they come from the highly poisonous "aqua regia" acids the boards are soaked in. Burning plastics and copper wire is also a polluting process, but one that should be distinguished from disassembly and repair, and from properly performed recycling. Arsenic in the river by Guiyu probably came from virgin copper mining upstream. There are risks in e-waste recycling, but the toxics have been dramatically overstated. . . .

FAST FACT

According to the US Environmental Protection Agency, 1 million recycled cell phones can yield 35,274 pounds of copper and 75 pounds of gold.

Myth: E-waste Recycling Isn't Worth It.

The Pitch: Freakonomics postulates that if recycling costs money, it cannot be done by the free market. Are e-waste programs just an expensive boondoggle? Clients cannot see the difference in service between a recycling company that charges them for the same pile of computers that another company pays for. It's all a cynical ploy to get you to pay to recycle something that does no harm in the dump.

This is the most dangerous myth because it stabs recycling programs in the heart—by reducing participation. EPA [the US Environmental Protection Agency], USGS [the US Geological Survey], the Department of Commerce, and state and county governments have studied recycling. We have weighed the costs and benefits, and set up programs. Convincing people NOT to participate creates a double waste—the material that gets thrown away as well as the cost of driving past a non-participant. By not participating, the cynics make recycling slightly less affordable and practical than it would otherwise be. . . .

Last year [2009], my [recycling] company managed about 5 million pounds of used TVs, computers, printers, VCRs, laptops, keyboards,

Monitors Made with Less-Harmful Materials Are Becoming More Popular

This graph shows how one electronics manufacturer, Sony, has seen its sales of CRT monitors decline as sales of LCD monitors increase. LCD monitors are not made with the hazardous metal cadmium.

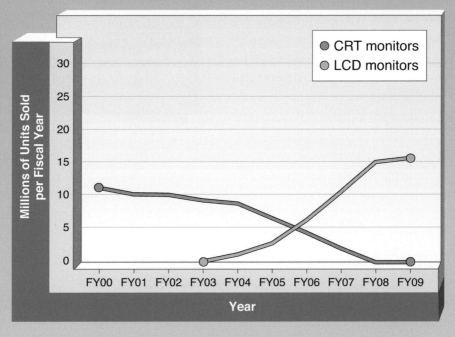

Taken from: Bill Harris. *Dubious Quality* (blog), May 19, 2010 (Data is from SONY annual reports).
http://dubiousquality.blogspot.com/2010/05/console-post-of-week-npds-and-sonys.html.

oscilloscopes, monitors, copy machines, cell phones, stereos, surge suppressors, and other surplus, working, repairable, junk and anything else you might label "e-waste." If you took all that material and put it in the dump, you'd avoid our fees (about 12 cents per pound after collection), about $600k. That 600k employs 25 people.

Most of the environmental harm from a disposable society is wasting the precious materials, which were extracted at great costs in environmentally sensitive areas. Gorilla extinction is tied to the mining of coltan for cell phones. Conflict metals are going into electronics as well as jewelry. Even non-toxic elements in a computer, such as tin, are mined at the expense of coral reefs in Indonesia. The copper production at the OK Tedi Mine in Papua, New Guinea, produces a green plume of cyanide tailings which is visible from outer space. Hard rock metal mining produces 45% of all toxics produced by all USA industries, and even more toxics in developing countries. 14 of the 15 largest Superfund [monies for cleaning up toxic waste dumps] sites come from virgin metal mining. Even the worst forms of recycling produce less pollution than the cleanest form of mining.

There are many more myths about e-waste. Is hard drive destruction demanded because Chinese paupers are booting up hard drives? Or is it the value of computer programs (MS Office, Photoshop, etc.) behind the legislation which drives shredding? Does a printer run through a shredder in the USA wind up in a different country than a printer exported for disassembly? Or does the fluff plastic and the steel just go into separate containers to the same place? Are cameras and ink cartridges refilled or burned? Do "green" products matter? Does just the promise to act green matter as much (through brand exposure and commitment) as the ecological footprint? There are many other sacred cows roaming El Rancho del E-Waste. I don't know, and am not ready to declare something a Myth if I'm not pretty confident in my facts. But that just means there is plenty more to research, study, and write about in the coming years.

EVALUATING THE AUTHOR'S ARGUMENTS:

Robin Ingenthron's viewpoint about the value of recycling is structured around what the author claims are misconceptions in the minds of those who disagree with him. In other words, rather than begin with his own arguments, he begins with the wrong ideas, or "myths," of others. What do you think are the strengths and limitations of this argumentative strategy?

Recycling Electronics Is Dangerous for the Environment and for Recycling Workers

"The e-waste dumped at Agbogbloshie has the capacity to seriously harm human health and the environment."

Osei Boateng

In the following viewpoint journalist Osei Boateng describes the dangers posed for workers in poor countries who take apart discarded electronic devices to extract and sell some of the valuable metals inside. Because consumers in wealthy countries like the United States are in the habit of replacing cell phones, computers, and other electronics every few years, he claims, an enormous amount of dangerous electronic waste—called "e-waste"—is generated and must be dealt with. Often, the cheapest way to get rid of old electronics is to ship it to poorer countries, and people in these countries, he concludes, are suffering from the environmental and public health dangers that wealthier countries can afford to avoid. Boateng is a special correspondent for *New African* magazine, where this viewpoint first appeared.

AS YOU READ, CONSIDER THE FOLLOWING QUESTIONS:
1. Why, according to the viewpoint, is much of the West's electronic waste not simply sent to local landfills?
2. About how much lead is contained in a typical cathode ray tube, as reported in the viewpoint?
3. Of the e-waste that Americans turn over to recyclers, what percentage is shipped overseas, according to the viewpoint?

Not many residents of Ghana's capital, Accra, go to the downmarket suburb of Agbogbloshie. But their health is sure to suffer from the toxic-laden smoke that spews into the atmosphere every day from a dump at Agbogbloshie where 15% of the world's e-waste is burned by young men who make a living out of metals scavenged from computers before they are set on fire.

According to Pieter Hugo's just published [2011] book, *Permanent Error*, Agbogbloshie is the new dumping ground for discarded computers, mobile phones, computer games, printers, and other gadgetry from the developed world, including the USA, UK, Canada, and the Netherlands.

Ghana's capital has thus become one of the largest repositories for toxic e-waste from around the world, which is burned by an army of unemployed young men engaged in a mad search for valuable metals such as copper, steel and aluminium, which they sell on the local market.

The e-waste is too toxic for most landfills in Western countries and so it is shipped "away" by fraudulent businesses posing as recyclers. But it turns the area in Accra into a poisonous wasteland contaminating the air, soil, and groundwater for miles around. . . .

An Ungreen Form of Recycling
According to [environmental activist Jim] Puckett, the Agbogbloshie dump is just one of the increasingly common inglorious final resting

A worker processes electronics at a recycling plant. So-called e-waste that is shipped to other countries to recycle puts those countries' environment and workers' health at risk, some experts contend.

places for some of the Western world's proudest products. It is here that the relics of the Information Age, with their miraculous microscopic circuits, transistors, capacitors, and semi-conductors are bludgeoned and torched with Stone Age technology. The residents at the Agbogbloshie dump make their living first by hauling and then by smashing, gutting, and burning the television sets and computers in a most ungreen form of 'recycling', to recover metals.

"This material," Puckett says, "made its arrival on African shores just some days earlier as cargo inside 40-foot intermodal corrugated containers. Around 400 of these, each containing about 600 computers or monitors, arrive each month at the Port of Tema, Ghana, from the UK, USA, Canada and countless other rich and developed countries.

"They may achieve a quick stay on the floors and shelves of hundreds of secondhand markets throughout Accra. But those that do not sell—about half, even if they work perfectly—are then picked up by small boys pushing heavy carts and hauled several miles to the outskirts of town, to be thrown away—to Agbogbloshie's scavengers."

In the last 30 years, the production and consumption of information technology has grown astronomically worldwide. As sales boom for computer games, printers, personal digital assistants (PDAs), electronic toys, MP3 players, digital cameras, GPS devices, camcorders and tablet readers, they come with a similarly unprecedented high rate of obsolescence. . . .

Mountains of Hazardous Waste

According to Puckett, the e-waste dumped at Agbogbloshie has the capacity to seriously harm human health and the environment. "A normal-sized cathode ray tube (CRT) contains around seven pounds of lead, a toxic metal, and the inside of the tube is coated with a toxic phosphor powder often containing cadmium compounds and toxic rare earth metals."

Puckett continues: "The circuit boards contain lead-tin solders, which are also toxic. The plastics are impregnated with brominated flame-retardants which are persistent chemicals of increasing concern, accumulating and persisting in our own bodies. Other toxic elements or chemicals found inside electronic equipment include mercury, beryllium, chromium, barium, selenium and polychlorinated biphenyls (PCBs). And thus the mountain ranges of e-waste arising on every continent represent an unforeseen toxic chemical crisis."

Electronics manufacturers in the developed world know that the only way they can maintain such staggering profits while addressing these troublesome waste mountains is to be seen as actively promoting recycling. But instead of seeking to produce longer-lived, upgradable products, they are encouraging the pattern of "buy, recycle, buy, recycle" in rapid succession.

As the problems mount, "governments in rich countries," says Puckett, "are slowly learning that e-waste is too toxic for most landfills, so they call for 'extended producer responsibility'—which means manufacturers must become financially and legally responsible for managing their products when they are no longer used.

"Therefore, all over the developed world, the idea of 'divert from landfill to recycling' has become policy—and increasingly, the law. But until recently, the manufacturers and governments cared little about what form that recycling would take or where it would happen."

As a result, the developed world's e-waste can migrate halfway around the world to be smashed and burned by young boys struggling to survive. In short, the international trade in toxic e-waste is driven by what economists call "cost externalisation"—a fancy term, Puckett says, "for finding somebody else to pay for a problem you created yourself".

"Externalising" the Problem

To maximise profits, Puckett reveals, many fraudulent businesses posing as recyclers "externalise" the costs by simply shipping the e-waste to poor countries which lack national infrastructure, environmental laws, enforcement and regulatory frameworks, and social safety nets.

"Sadly such dumping is the global norm, not the exception," Puckett points out. "In the US, it is estimated that about 80% of old computers, TVs and other electronic equipment given over to 'recyclers' are then simply exported. In Europe, the European Commission claims that 54% of the electronic waste stream is unaccounted for and likely goes to substandard treatment or export.

"In this way, the high-tech 'effluent of the affluent' is flooding the globe."

In Accra, the environmental journalist Mike Anane has been gathering the asset tags [identifying property] of the e-waste from the Agbogbloshie dump for several years. Puckett says: "Whenever I see such tags, I recall the words of a Los Angeles government official who, when asked by the *Los Angeles Times* where their old computers went, replied: 'I don't know where they go. They go away.' I found her agency's asset tags on old computers in the infamous e-waste dumping ground of Guiyu in China." . . .

Puckett insists that the primary responsibility lies with the exporting countries, a point agreed by [chemistry professor Oladele] Osibanjo.

Export of E-waste

Most of the exported electronic waste from the United States is sent to China for disposal or recycling.

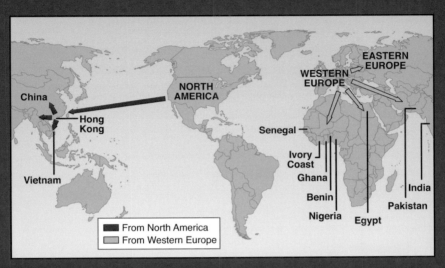

Taken from: Greenpeace, Basel Action Network. http://greenfudge.org/2010/09/13/uk-govt-and-european-e-waste-illegally-dumped-in-africa/.

"Hazardous wastes," the Nigerian says, "should never go from developed to developing countries. We live in a global village with a common destiny. We must be sure that all sides are safe at the end of the day."

Puckett has the last word, appealing to his people in the developed world: "Wherever we live, we must realise that when we sweep things out of our lives and throw them away . . . they don't ever disappear as we might like to believe. We must know that 'away' is in fact a place.

"In a world where cost externalisation is made all too easy by the pathways of globalisation, 'away' is likely to be somewhere people are impoverished, disenfranchised, powerless, and too desperate to resist the poison for the realities of their poverty. 'Away' is likely to be a place where people and environments will suffer for our carelessness, our ignorance or indifference. Away is a place called Agbogbloshie."

EVALUATING THE AUTHOR'S ARGUMENTS:

In the viewpoint you have just read, the author is clear about the dangers that the workers who dismantle electronics are exposed to, and he is also clear that he believes it is not fair for people in poor countries to face risks created by people in wealthier countries. Whom do you think the author holds to blame for this injustice: the consumers who buy new electronics every few years, the manufacturers who encourage consumers to buy new devices before the old ones wear out, the recyclers who send electronics overseas, governments that have not made laws to regulate e-waste, or someone else? Who do you think should be responsible for protecting people and the environment from electronic waste?

Chapter 3

How Can Consumers Reduce the Amount of Plastic Waste Generated?

A veritable mountain of plastic waits to be recycled. Whether the amount of plastic waste generated can be reduced is often debated.

Viewpoint

1

Bottled Water Should Be Banned

Jean Hill, as told to ConcordConserves.org

"Bottled water has so many problems that it is time to do something meaningful about it."

The following viewpoint is an interview with Jean Hill, a resident of Concord, Massachusetts, who has campaigned since 2010 through the city's local system—including town meetings, articles, and bylaws—to have sales of single-serve bottled water banned in Concord. Hill argues that bottled water wastes resources, contributes to global climate change, and generates large numbers of bottles that are not recycled. Because bottled water is such a harmful and unnecessary product, she claims, banning it, even while allowing sales of other bottled beverages, will have a clear impact on people's habits and attitudes. Eventually, she concludes, Concord's ban might inspire other communities to enact their own. The interview was conducted by the staff of ConcordConserves.org, a website working to reduce human impact on the environment through education, communication, and online tools.

  1. According to the viewpoint, what kinds of groups have already limited or eliminated their purchases of bottled water?
  2. Why does Jean Hill believe that banning the sale of single-serve bottled water will not harm local businesses, according to the viewpoint?
  3. How will the proposed law affect events during which people give away bottled water, according to the viewpoint?

I sat down with Jean Hill at her home the other day and we talked about the up-and-coming Town Meeting [March 7, 2011] and Article 38 which [would ban the sale of single-serve bottled water in Concord, Massachusetts]. I asked her to tell me how this all started.

Would you tell me a little bit about yourself and how you got started as an activist?

Jean Hill: When I was sixteen and World War II was raging, I wanted to serve my country in some way, particularly since my Dad was in the U.S. Navy and fighting in the war. I got a summer job working in a factory that had been converted to manufacturing parachutes. There were many permanent workers who had worked there for many years, yet had never had a paid vacation. I believed this to be unjust so I tried to start a union. I went to the union office in Times Square, N.Y., where the factory was located, and told the officials there of my plan. They brushed me off because they thought I was a smart aleck kid. This was my first attempt at speaking out against injustice.

Why is this Bylaw proposed under Article 38 important?

Well, it's important because bottled water has so many problems that it is time to do something meaningful about it. It is an enormous waste of resources; it pollutes our waterways and harms wildlife; it contributes to global warming; it harms local communities; it is NOT safer than our own water; it is just not right. Enough is enough.

Also, bottled water doesn't fit with our community values. We're a smart community of people who cannot be tricked by clever marketing. And we are not willing to put convenience ahead of our concern for the near and long-term consequences of bottled water.

The momentum is growing in the national movement against bottled water. Many cities, towns and states have prohibited government purchases; many colleges and universities have virtually eliminated bottled water from campus. Concord's decision to ban the sale of bottled water in town will set a legal precedent, bringing action to the next level and helping other communities move forward.

Isn't this just a recycling issue? What if we all recycled all plastic water bottles?

Bottled water is much more than a recycling issue. Even if we recycled all bottles, bottled water would still cause harm to the environment in the form of fossil fuel use and carbon dioxide emissions. And bottled water would still be a virtually unregulated, costly and unjust product. We need to reduce the amount of trash in the world and part of that is reducing the amount of bottles of water out there, not recycling them.

Won't this hurt our local businesses?

I believe this Bylaw will have minimal impact on local businesses. Bottled water is one of many hundreds of products sold in these stores. And the stores will still be able to sell other types of beverages and larger sizes of bottled water if they choose. I have asked some of our local businesses in town what portion of their business includes the sale of single-serve bottled water and they replied it is a very, very, very small portion of their business. Also, many businesses already provide tap water to their customers. I think our local businesses care about the environment and want to provide good products to our community.

FAST FACT

Americans throw away 25 million plastic beverage bottles every hour, according to the Curbside Value Partnership.

Won't people just go to neighboring towns to buy bottled water?

Yes, that's possible, but what I'm trying to do with this Bylaw is to increase the barriers to buying single-serve bottled water because in order to help people change, you need to put policies in place that steer them away from buying bottled water and toward considering the many other good alternatives. This, I hope, will make people stop and think before grabbing that bottle of water. Instead, I'd love

Critics say that using bottled water not only generates large amounts of plastic waste that is not recycled but also contributes to global warming.

to see people bringing their own tap water from home in their reusable bottles. There are some very nice ones out there that I'd highly recommend. It not only saves people money, but also is good for the environment and reduces trash. And if Concord is successful in passing this Bylaw, I hope that other towns will consider taking action too.

Why does the Article focus on single-serving-sized bottles and not all bottled water?

This is the size that most people purchase and it has the greatest impact on the environment in terms of energy use and carbon dioxide emissions. Getting rid of this size would have a large impact and it's a good start for the Bylaw.

Exactly what is and what is not included in the Bylaw?

It includes single-serve (1 liter or less) polyethylene terephthalate (PET) containers of plain drinking water in all of its forms—spring

Bottled Water: A Recycling Issue?

According to the International Bottled Water Association, 30.9% of the PET bottles that bottled water is sold in are recycled, making those bottles the nation's most recycled plastic container.

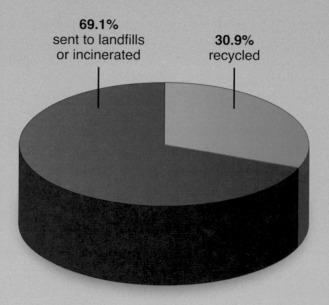

69.1%
sent to landfills
or incinerated

30.9%
recycled

Taken from: IBWA, 2012. www.bottledwater.org/news/ibwa-rebuts-misleading-and-factually-incorrect-video-about-bottled-water#.

water, artesian water, ground water, mineral water, purified water, sterile water and well water. The Bylaw does not apply to sparkling water, flavored water, sports drinks (e.g., Gatorade), milk, juice, tea and soda.

It does not apply to PET containers of drinking water greater than 1 liter in size, and other types of containers (e.g., paper, glass) of any size drinking water. Also, the Bylaw refers to sales of single-serve bottled water in Concord, not situations in which bottled water is given away, although I hope that people switch to providing tap water.

What is your hope for the future if/when this Bylaw is passed?

I am hoping that this will be a call to action to other towns and states that will also start restricting single-serve bottled water purchases, and that will eventually lead to a reduction in wasted resources, pollution of waterways and wildlife, and global warming. I'm very concerned for our resources and feel we need to conserve them as much as possible now. I know this town is full of well-educated people who look at the big picture and care about the impact of today's choices. I am counting on them to be people who will take meaningful action on a serious issue.[1]

Are you planning any more Bylaws for the future?
Next, I may tackle the plastic bag issue!

EVALUATING THE AUTHOR'S ARGUMENTS:

In the viewpoint you have just read, Jean Hill, the subject of the interview, describes the people of Concord, Massachusetts, as "a smart community of people who cannot be tricked" and "well-educated people who look at the big picture." What effect do you think phrases like these would have on readers from Concord? How might the effect be different on readers from other places?

---

1. A 2012 version of the bylaw passed in Concord. As of June 1, 2012, the town was waiting to see whether the state attorney general would approve the bylaw and the ban.

Viewpoint 2

Banning Bottled Water Will Not Significantly Help the Environment

Charles Fishman

"How is the fleet of trucks delivering water in bottles any different than the fleets delivering caramel-colored, caffeinated water in bottles?"

In the following viewpoint journalist Charles Fishman argues that bottled water is an expensive and unnecessary product but that banning it would not accomplish what well-meaning supporters of banning expect. Bottled water bans that do not address other beverages, he points out, and ignore the fact that energy drinks and sodas are made up of mostly water. These other beverages require similar amounts of energy to make and to transport, he claims, and come in the same plastic bottles as water. Colleges that consider banning bottled water, he concludes, should instead direct their attention to educating students to make wise decisions about what they drink. Fishman is an award-winning investigative journalist and the author of *The Big Thirst* (2011).

AS YOU READ, CONSIDER THE FOLLOWING QUESTIONS:
1. How many colleges and universities in the United States and Canada have banned the sale of bottled water, as reported in the viewpoint?
2. How does the price of tap water compare with the price of bottled water, according to the viewpoint?
3. What improvement does the viewpoint suggest cities might make to help citizens rely less on bottled water?

I remember the moment when the silliness of bottled water became vividly clear to me. I was standing in the factory in San Pellegrino, Italy, at the foot of the Italian Alps, where San Pellegrino water is sealed in those shapely green bottles.

Leave aside that the glass bottles weigh more than the water they contain, or the journey those bottles of water have to make, by truck and ship and truck again, to land on a grocery shelf or café table in Manhattan or St. Louis.

The bottles themselves have to be washed before being filled. And as Pellegrino's wizened factory operations manager explained, they wash the bottles with . . . Pellegrino water. Before filling them with Pellegrino water.

Of course they do.

But then the silliness took a leap. Where, I asked, do the bubbles in Pellegrino come from? The plant manager's eyes lit up. Pellegrino water comes out of the ground uncarbonated, in fact. Pellegrino has another spring to the south in central Italy that is naturally carbonated. The company harvests the carbon dioxide from that spring, purifies it, compresses it, trucks it north to Pellegrino, and injects it into the water as part of the bottling process.

No matter how far your Pellegrino water has traveled to get to you, the dancing Italian bubbles that make it so delightful have traveled just a little farther.

A Product No One Needs

San Pellegrino, which is now owned by the conglomerate Nestlé, has a storied history—as a town, as a spring, as a water—but let's be clear:

It's a product no one needs. It's refreshing, it's appealing, but it is a pure indulgence. Whether you live in Milan, just down the road, or Mexico City, where Pellegrino is on the shelves at Wal-Mart. And I say that as someone whose wife and 13-year-old son both love San Pellegrino.

In fact, unless you're struggling in the aftermath of a natural disaster, unless you live in a developing world nation without safe tap water, all bottled water really falls into that category: luxury, indulgence, convenience.

That's okay, of course, lots of things I like are indulgences: Oreos, *The Good Wife*, Italian Merlot, even the ice cubes I all-but-require in the glass of water that sits on my desk through the work day.

There is a fresh burst of controversy about bottled water on college campuses, specifically, around whether bottled water should be sold in the dining halls of U.S. and Canadian universities. Last week [February 2012], the University of Vermont became the latest of 15 campuses in the U.S. and Canada to ban the sale of bottled water, according to figures from the Association for the Advancement of Sustainability in Higher Education (AASHE).

Dozens more campuses have active campaigns to discourage bottled water purchases—including giving out free reuseable water bottles to students, and providing elegant, easy-to-use bottle filling stations. (Try to fill a water bottle from a water fountain sometime—you'll be lucky to get halfway full.)

Over the weekend [February 12, 2012], NPR's [National Public Radio] food blog had a story about college students squaring off against the bottled water industry which drew more than 100 comments. Columbia University's Water Center posted an essay last week asking, "Should Universities Ban Bottled Water?" which is getting a little Twitter attention.

The essay doesn't answer the question, but I will: Of course bottled water shouldn't be banned.

Virtually all the bans are the result of well-intentioned student activism on campus.

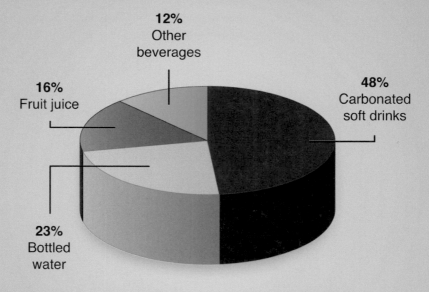

Bottled Water Not the Major Source of PET Bottles

According to 2008 data from the United Kingdom, bottled water accounts for only 23% of the PET bottles used annually.

12%
Other
beverages

16%
Fruit juice

48%
Carbonated
soft drinks

23%
Bottled
water

Taken from: "Light Weight PET Bottles," ITWMima Packaging Systems, February 19, 2010. www.stretch-wrap-machines.co.uk/?page=ITWMimaNews&article=41.

But I don't understand how campuses can ban sales of bottled water while continuing to sell Coke, Pepsi, Mountain Dew, Vitamin Water and Red Bull.

What do the fired-up campus environmentalists think Coke is, anyway? Regular Coke is about 95 percent water; Diet Coke is 99 percent water.

Faulty, but Well-Intentioned, Reasoning

The reasoning runs something like this: Water is available on campus—from taps, from spigots, from filtered water-filling stations. Students and staff don't need it delivered in plastic bottles. Coke and Red Bull aren't available the same way. (Although sodas, of course, are often delivered on tap in dining halls.)

The author claims that banning bottled water will not help reduce garbage unless all other beverages, which are mostly water and come in bottles, too, are banned as well.

The environmental contrail from bottled water (which I wrote about in a magazine story that took me to both Fiji and Poland Spring, Maine) is astonishing. It takes a fleet equivalent to 40,000 18-wheelers just to deliver the bottled water Americans buy every week.

But how is the fleet of trucks delivering water in bottles any different than the fleets delivering caramel-colored, caffeinated water in bottles? It takes 2.5 liters of water to produce every liter of Coke products.

I can understand cities banning the purchase of bottled water with city funds for city offices—as San Francisco, Seattle, and New York have done. That's about both money and symbolism. Those cities run tap water systems—why would their employees need bottled water paid for by taxpayers?

I can understand vigorous on-campus awareness efforts to create a culture where carrying a bottle of Evian or Deer Park or Smart Water into class causes raised eyebrows. (No college student appears to be able to make it through a class these days without a drink of some kind—coffee, soda, water—as if scholarship had become seriously dehydrating. Not so long ago, students wouldn't have thought of stepping into a lecture hall with a cup of coffee or a can of soda.)

Indeed, you can start with the fact that buying water in a bottle makes absolutely no economic sense. The water in a half-liter bottle typically costs 3,000 times what the same amount of water from a spigot costs. Buy a single bottle of Poland Spring for $1.29 at the college store, and you can refill the bottle every day for 8 years—college plus medical school!—before the tap water costs what the original Poland Spring cost.

The very university food service systems that proudly announce bottled water bans offer products with at least as much environmental impact that also have all kinds of dietary impact. Froot Loops at breakfast? Chocolate chip cookies at dinner? Frozen yogurt on tap 16 hours a day?

Bottled water bans are not just oddly hypocritical—taking bottled water out of campus vending machines while leaving soda in those machines—they seem oddly misplaced in a setting where people are supposed to be thinking for themselves.

I love seeing college students leading an imaginative revival of the drinking fountain—and it would be great if the revival spilled beyond campuses into cities. Why do people buy bottled water? Because cities don't have public water fountains that are easy to use, clean and safe.

The bottled water debates is a great way of waking people up to the big water issues almost every community faces—scarcity, purity, reuse, sustainability. But the conversation has to move on from bottled water to the water supply itself.

Banning bottled water doesn't really teach anyone anything.

Viewpoint

3

Recyclable Bioplastics Can Reduce Plastic Waste

Scott Vitters, as told to Melanie D.G. Kaplan

"For our containers, recycling is better than biodegradable because you can reclaim the energy and use it again and again."

In the following viewpoint Coca-Cola executive Scott Vitters is interviewed by journalist Melanie D.G. Kaplan about the development and potential of a new plastic bottle, the PlantBottle, which is made partially from plant materials. Vitters argues that his company's bottle is superior to other plastic bottles that claim to be environmentally friendly because the plants used in production are grown using sustainable practices and because Coca-Cola has taken steps to ensure the bottles are recycled. Recyclable plastic bottles are a better choice than biodegradable, he claims, because using recyclables again and again saves energy.

AS YOU READ, CONSIDER THE FOLLOWING QUESTIONS:

1. What was the problem with some of the existing plant-based materials Coca-Cola tried before the company found the current way of making bottles, according to the viewpoint?
2. What plant is used to make the plastic bottles described in the viewpoint?
3. Where is the world's largest bottle-to-bottle recycling plant, according to the viewpoint?

You wouldn't know it from looking at them on the grocery store shelf (and you'd need carbon-14 dating tools to make an accurate identification), but Coca-Cola's recyclable PlantBottle PET [polyethylene terephthalate] plastic bottles are an innovative and ground-breaking step in the food and beverage industry. Up to 30 percent of the PlantBottle materials are derived from plants, and the company's goal is to eventually roll out bottles that are made 100 percent from renewable raw materials, and still fully recyclable.

I recently spoke with Scott Vitters, general manager of Coca-Cola's PlantBottle Packaging Platform. He explained why it's better to have a recyclable bottle than a biodegradable one; how bottles recycle into chairs; and how the manufacturer is now relying on sugar for something other than sweetening its carbonated beverages.

[Melanie D. G. Kaplan:] One-third of your PlantBottle is made from plant-based materials. Explain how that works.

[Scott Vitters:] When you look at the chemistry of PET plastic, think of it as two key ingredients. We have today been able to figure out how to replace one of those ingredients, which is by weight 30 percent of the bottle. When you look at 30 percent of all our packaging, that's a tremendous shift.

In a lab, we've already demonstrated an ability to do the other 70 percent. Our strategy is to roll out PlantBottle at 30 percent throughout the world while we are working on the technology for the other ingredient.

And recycling?

There is no other bottle in the marketplace today that is made with plants, fully recyclable and capable of meeting our quality requirements. There are other bottles made with plants, and they may be claiming to be recyclable, but is there a commercial market to recycle it? . . .

Are some Coca-Cola products more compatible with PlantBottle than others?

That was [a] key driving principle for us—a number of the existing plant-based materials could only be used with water, and even those—no pun intended—didn't hold water. So we wanted to find a material that could be used for all our products. We've launched it across our product platforms. Our ultimate goal is to have it in 100 percent [of] our packages by 2020.

At a press conference, executives from various companies announce their partnership to produce the first bioplastic bottle made from recyclable plant material.

What we are making is the exact same plastic we're using today. The only way to tell a difference is if you do carbon-14 dating—you can look at the source of the carbon and see whether it's from fossil fuels or not. . . .

The plant part of your PlantBottle is made from sugar and molasses. What is the source for those ingredients?

Just because you make a product from plants doesn't mean it's better for the environment. You have to look at the energy input, the water use, fertilizers, growing, the total harvesting of the product … and ask, is it truly better for the environment than what we're using today? We spent more than a year specifically looking at that issue. Coke was the first in the food and beverage industry to develop life cycle analysis in the late '60s to guide our decision-making; it has been a cornerstone of our program.

Today, for this program, we've only approved one agricultural feedstock: sugar cane and molasses from Brazil. The types of plants used and the places they are grown made a big difference on environmental performance. Brazilian sugar cane—it's mostly rain-fed, so you have very little irrigation; and you have mainly organic fertilizers.

Our commitment is to depend not only on Brazilian sugar cane. We are advancing using the solutions that use the waste from plants—bark or stems or husks—and being able to turn that into the [recyclable plastic bottles]. . . .

Can you describe the process and behind-the-scenes of developing PlantBottle?

You have to go back to the 2002 Olympics in Salt Lake. We had rolled out a bioplastic cup at the time, and we were really looking at advancing renewable and recyclable materials for our business. We had a desire around this goal of decoupling PET growth from fossil fuels as well as waste generation. We kept looking at materials, but either they weren't recyclable or didn't meet our standards in another way.

We had this tension in the company for a while—marketing wanted plant-based plastic, but grounded in the reality that there were environmental concerns and technical limitations: At the time the materials didn't deliver the environmental benefits. But instead of compromising we ended up discovering that we could start making plant-based plastic using the same type of plastic we were using today, as recyclable as PET plastic. That was a major breakthrough—not only for us but for the industry, in terms of realizing we could move to a new material.

There were paradigms that needed to be shifted on what truly was better for the environment—one was a focus on biodegradable. I still get the question a lot: "Is it biodegradable," with the assumption that biodegradable would be better. The reality is that for our containers, recycling is better than biodegradable because you can reclaim the energy and use it again and again, rather than having it make a single trip and then just go back in the dirt.

It sounds really good—made from nature, back to nature. But for plastic bottles, it is much preferable to recover the material and use

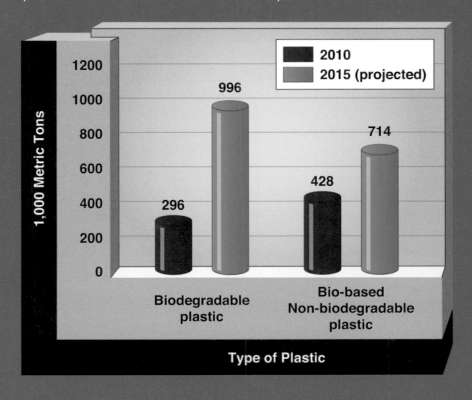

Bioplastics: Global Production Capacity

Between 2010 and 2015, the capacity for factories around the world to produce biodegradable and bio-based non-biodegradable recyclable plastics is expected to more than double. Non-biodegradable bio-based plastic includes the PlantBottle and other plant-based containers.

1,000 Metric Tons (y-axis)

Legend:
- 2010
- 2015 (projected)

Biodegradable plastic: 296 (2010), 996 (2015 projected)
Bio-based Non-biodegradable plastic: 428 (2010), 714 (2015 projected)

Type of Plastic (x-axis)

Taken from: European Bioplastics/University of Applied Sciences and Arts, Hanover, 2011. http://en.european -bioplastics.org/press/press-pictures/labelling-logos-charts/.

it again and again. So it's not about designing it to be biodegradable. It's about making a closed loop.

People were trying to innovate an entirely new plastic, which was throwing out all the advantages of the existing plastic—a material that is very efficient: It holds carbonation and protects product quality; consumers love its weight and shatter-resistance; it's resealable. However, it's still based on non-renewable petro-chemical resources.

So we said the challenge is not to throw out all those advantages, but how do you build on those advantages by making it renewable.

As consumers have gotten more engaged in green marketing, it's easier to communicate stories by focusing on one attribute—the lightest packaging, the most plant-based material. Those are all attributes that could lead to better environmental performance. But if it's so lightweight that in shipping the product breaks and you have to double the secondary packaging—that's not necessarily better.

What is the end market for the bottles?

Have you seen the Navy 111 Chair? It's an iconic design chair made from 111 recycled Coke bottles. We also have a merchandise line made out of recycled products, mostly to engage and inspire consumers. We've also been building bottle-to-bottle recycling technologies, which is the closed loop cycle we hope to advance.

Where is that bottle-to-bottle recycling plant?

Over a year ago we opened in Spartanburg, South Carolina, the largest bottle-to-bottle recycling facility in the world.

Our first plant we invested in was in Australia. It's one thing to say you want to use recycled material. It's another thing to build the infrastructure.

How many PlantBottles were produced last year?

2.5 billion. We believe that this is the future.

EVALUATING THE AUTHOR'S ARGUMENTS:

The viewpoint you have just read is an interview with Scott Vitters, an executive from a profit-making company. In such a position, Vitters must present himself as knowledgeable and fair while presenting his company in the best possible light. How well does he manage this tension? How does his position with the company he is describing affect how you read his arguments?

Viewpoint
4

Bioplastics Make Recycling Programs More Complicated

"Bioplastics are causing problems for both plastics recyclers and for commercial composting facilities because they are often wrongly sorted."

Mary Catherine O'Connor

In the following viewpoint journalist Mary Catherine O'Connor describes the difficulties that arise when bioplastics are disposed of by well-meaning but confused consumers. Because bioplastics are so new—and because some of the thirteen bioplastics being used are recyclable while others are compostable—consumers often do not know what to do with their plastic trash. This confusion, O'Connor claims, can lead to compostable plastics contaminating recyclable plastics at a recycling plant, sending large batches of ruined material to the landfill. Until consumers and recyclers become more familiar with the new plastics, she concludes, mistakes will be made, and much of the new bioplastics will end up in landfills. O'Connor covers environmental sustainability, technology, and other topics for leading publications.

AS YOU READ, CONSIDER THE FOLLOWING QUESTIONS:

1. What does the number 7 on a piece of plastic trash indicate, according to the viewpoint?
2. What is the meaning of the term *bioplastic*, as explained in the viewpoint?
3. Why do most recycling facilities not use infrared sensors to separate PLA from PET, according to the viewpoint?

You're standing in front of three bins—one for compost, one for recycling and one for landfill—holding an empty container called a "PlantBottle" and a clear plastic cup embossed with the recycling triangle and the number seven. Now what?

Your instinct might be to put that "PlantBottle" in the compost bin, and to put the clear plastic cup in the recycling bin. But in this case, you'd be wrong on both counts.

PlantBottle is Coca-Cola's brand for its bio-based plastic bottles, and while they are made either partially or wholly from plant-derived materials, they have the identical chemical structure of plastic made from oil, and therefore should be recycled right along with petro-derived plastic. A PlantBottle, despite its name, can't be composted.

And the cup bearing the recycling logo and the number seven? Seven is the catchall for plastics that aren't generally recyclable but that a few curbside systems might take—things like durable goods such as sunglasses, DVDs and some types of rugged plastic packaging. Compostable plastic is lumped under number seven, too. This cup in your hand happens to be a compostable bioplastic material, PLA [corn plastic], and so, though it might seem counterintuitive, it is supposed to go in the compost bin. Of course, if the word "compostable" were printed on the cup, this would be obvious. But such hints are not always provided.

If this all seems confusing, that's because it is. But we're here to shine a light on bioplastic packaging and its end-of-life story, because you'll be seeing more and more of it in the coming years. Any sustainable business worth its weight in wheatgrass is starting to use bioplastic packaging. And within the packaging industry, this stuff is the new black. The market for bioplastics is forecast to grow at an average annual rate of about 25 percent through 2015, with production reaching 884,000 tons by 2020.

Chicken feathers are used to make some so-called bioplastic products. Of the thirteen bioplastics now in use, some are recyclable while others are compostable, which has led to confusion among consumers about how to recycle their plastic trash.

Making Plastics Disappear?

Set against the haunting images of our plastic-choked oceans and landscapes, and considering the pathetically low recycling rates in the US (only about 30 percent of polyethylene terephthalate, or PET, bottles are collected for recycling), the rise of bioplastics seems, at first glance, encouraging. With municipalities across the country banning standard, petroleum-based, single-use plastics and some mandating residential composting, more businesses and consumers are looking for plastic packaging that will, *poof!*, disappear once its short, useful life is over.

But—spoiler alert—that's not actually how it all works.

For one thing, bioplastics vary widely in terms of both their base material and their ability (or inability) to biodegrade. For another, bioplastics are causing problems for both plastics recyclers and for commercial composting facilities because they are often wrongly sorted. . . .

What Is Bioplastic?

First, let's start with a primer on the term "bioplastic." Basically, a bioplastic is a polymer made—wholly or in part—from a renewable, plant-based feedstock. There are some exceptions to this rule, such as Ecoflex, a bioplastic made from petrochemicals. It earns its "bioplastic" label from the fact that it will biodegrade when placed in a commercial composting system. As you can see, the term bioplastic is quite broad.

FAST FACT

Only two companies in the world have facilities to recycle PLA, or corn plastic, the most common bioplastic packaging material; one is in Wisconsin, and the other is in Europe.

Some bioplastics are designed such that microorganisms inside a compost pile will completely consume them within a relatively short period of time. Other bioplastics will decompose under certain conditions, but they will not do so quickly or completely enough to be considered compostable. Some producers claim their packaging is biodegradable, when in reality it just contains additives that make the plastic break down into small pellets.

Cartoon for "What's Up with Recyclable Plastics," by Slug Signorino, *The Straight Dope,* December 30, 2009.
Copyright © 2009 by Slug Signorino. All rights reserved. Reproduced by permission.

So it's very important to note that "bio-based," "biodegradable" and "compostable" are individual attributes. A given bioplastic might be all three of these things—for example a bioplastic called polylactic acid (PLA) made from corn by the Cargill-owned Nature Works company; or it might only be one of these things—such as the PET or high-density polyethylene (HDPE) PlantBottle that is bio-based (and recyclable) but not biodegradable or compostable.

Given this morass of feedstocks and end-of-life options, it's impossible to chart the lifecycle of bioplastics as a group; it must be done per material. That isn't easy given there are around 13 different bioplastics in use today. . . .

Everything in Its Not-So-Right Place

Which brings us back to the confusion at the recycling bin. For argument's sake, let's say you put the PET PlantBottle in the compost bin (a reasonable mistake) and put the mystery cup in the recycle bin (after all, it looks and feels like normal plastic). Then what?

Unless it gets hand-sorted, that PLA cup is likely going to end up in the PET stream in a recycling facility, where it doesn't belong. And that PET PlantBottle will go to a composting facility, where it'll be rooted out and sent to the landfill instead of being recycled.

Back at the recycling facility, PLA can be mechanically separated from PET using an infrared sensor. But recyclers don't usually take the trouble to do such sorting. It's an expensive process and no one is going to pay them enough for that PLA to justify the cost, explains David Cornell, technical director of the Association of Postconsumer Plastic Recyclers.

Within the PET stream, PLA tends to muck things up. If enough PLA (or other non-PET material) ends up in a bale of PET, a plastics reclaimer is going to turn it away and the bale will likely end up in a landfill. So suddenly those earth-friendly packaging materials have cut short the possibility that the PET inside that bale will find another useful life before ending up in a landfill. (Most PET is downcycled into other products, such as clothing or construction material, rather than truly recycled, due to the complexity and cost of turning PET back into PET.)

But even if the PLA and PET are put in their proper bins, one can argue that the recyclable PET's end of life scenario is better than compostable PLA's. For one thing, the composting facility is likely to pull that PLA cup out of the compost material and trash it. "Anything that looks like plastic is a problem to composters," Cornell says, because they can't easily discern whether a material is a compostable bioplastic when it's moving quickly past on a conveyor belt.…

As a result of this disconnect, you might be dutifully placing compostable plastic into a municipal compost collection bin (assuming you live in one of the few U.S. cities that currently provides this type of curbside collection) only to have the commercial composter pull it out of the stream and divert it to the landfill.

That's a nasty carbon footprint for those eco-containers.

EVALUATING THE AUTHOR'S ARGUMENTS:

One of the points of the viewpoint that you have just read is that the language used to describe what happens to garbage can be confusing. O'Connor demonstrates that there are important distinctions between "PET" and "PLA," between "biodegradable" and "compostable," and between "recycling" and "downcycling." How well does she do at sorting out this language for her readers? Why might she be willing to leave readers somewhat confused about the terms?

Facts About Garbage and Recycling

Editor's note: These facts can be used in reports to add credibility when making important points or claims.

American Attitudes About Recycling

In April 2012 a group called Call2Recycle surveyed American adults about their attitudes about environmental responsibility. Among the findings:

- Eighty-four percent said they have recycled in the past year to help the environment.
- More than half, or 57 percent, said that they have old electronics at home that could be recycled. The electronics included cell phones (46 percent of respondents), computers (33 percent), and televisions (25 percent).
- When asked what makes recycling difficult, 44 percent said that they do not know how or where to recycle electronics, while 19 percent said no local store accepts electronics for recycling.
- In 2009, 12 percent of respondents said that they suffer from "green guilt," or a concern that they should be doing more to help the environment; in 2012, 29 percent reported feeling "green guilt."

A 2010 Rasmussen poll asked Americans about lifestyle changes needed to protect the environment. The poll found:

- Of those surveyed, 51 percent believed that major lifestyle cutbacks are needed to help the environment; 32 percent disagreed; 16 percent were undecided.
- Sixty-five percent said that Americans will not be willing to make the needed cutbacks; 17 percent said Americans would make those changes; 18 percent were not sure.
- Seventy-nine percent said that they believe Americans are more environmentally aware than they were twenty-five years ago; 13 percent disagreed.

The Gallup organization surveys Americans in March every few years about actions they take to be environmentally friendly. The 2010 Gallup survey showed little change from the 2000 survey:

- In 2010, 90 percent of respondents said that they had voluntarily recycled newspapers, glass, aluminum, motor oil, or other items; in 2000, the number was also 90 percent.
- In 2010, 76 percent said that they had bought a product specifically because they believed it was better for the environment; in 2000, 73 percent said they had done this.
- In response to a new question introduced in 2010, 70 percent said that they used reusable shopping bags at the grocery store instead of the store's plastic or paper bags.

Recycling in Practice

According to the Aluminum Association:

- About 119,482 cans are recycled every minute nationwide.
- If lined up end to end, the 62.6 billion cans recycled in 2010 would stretch 171 times around the equator.

As reported by the Glass Packaging Institute:

- Glass containers are 100 percent recyclable. A glass container can be recycled an infinite number of times with no loss in quality.
- Approximately 80 percent of glass containers submitted for recycling are made into new glass bottles.
- In 2010, more than 41 percent of glass soft drink and beer bottles were recycled.
- In 2010, 47 percent of the glass bottles in Minnesota were recycled; more than 80 percent were recycled in California.
- Recycling one glass bottle saves enough energy to power a one-hundred-watt lightbulb for four hours, a computer for thirty minutes, or a television for twenty minutes.

According to Earth911.com's reporting on paper recycling:

- Approximately 254 million (86 percent) of Americans have access to paper recycling programs, either at their own curbs or at drop-off sites.
- More than 37 percent of the fiber used to make new paper products in the United States comes from recycled sources.

- Every ton of paper recycled saves more than 3.3 cubic yards of landfill space.
- If all of the Sunday newspapers printed in the United States were recycled, about 26 million trees would be saved each year.

The Steel Recycling Institute reports:
- Steel is the most-recycled material in the United States. Each year, more steel is recycled in the United States than paper, plastic, aluminum and glass combined.
- For at least five decades, more than 50 percent of the steel produced in this country has been recycled through the steelmaking process. In 2010, 88 percent of steel was recycled.
- In 1988, about 15 percent of steel cans were recycled; in 2010, more than 67 percent were recycled.
- In 1988, about 20 percent of the steel in appliances was recycled; in 2010, the figure was 90 percent.

Waste in the United States

According to the National Solid Wastes Management Association and the Waste Equipment Technology Association:
- America's waste industry successfully manages nearly 545 million tons of solid waste each year. This waste is equal to the weight of more than 5,600 Nimitz Class aircraft carriers, 247,000 space shuttles, or 2.3 million Boeing 747 jumbo jets.
- If all of the solid waste collected in the United States in one year were put in a line of average garbage trucks, that line of trucks could cross the country from New York City to Los Angeles more than one hundred times.
- An average kitchen-size bag of trash contains enough energy to light a one-hundred-watt lightbulb for more than twenty-four hours.

Organizations to Contact

The editors have compiled the following list of organizations concerned with the issues debated in this book. The descriptions are derived from materials provided by the organizations. All have publications or information available for interested readers. The list was compiled on the date of publication of the present volume; the information provided here may change. Be aware that many organizations take several weeks or longer to respond to inquiries, so allow as much time as possible for the receipt of requested materials.

American Chemistry Council (ACC)
700 Second St. NE
Washington, DC 20002
(202) 249-7000
websites: http://plastics.americanchemistry.com/Sustainability -Recycling; http://plasticbagfacts.org

The ACC is a trade organization representing American chemical companies, including plastics manufacturers. Through various websites it offers information about the role of plastics in garbage and recycling. A "Sustainability-Recycling" page discusses ways to reduce, reuse, recycle, and recover plastics; it also includes educational resources and plastic statistics. The ACC also sponsors the Progressive Bag Affiliates, which hosts a website dedicated to the benefits of plastic bags.

American Forest & Paper Association (AF&PA)
1111 Nineteenth St. NW, Ste. 800
Washington, DC 20036
website: www.paperrecycles.org

The AF&PA is the national trade association of the forest products industry, representing forest landowners as well as manufacturers of pulp, paper, packaging, and wood products. The AF&PA sponsors PaperRecycles.org, a website dedicated to presenting information about recycling paper in the workplace, schools, and communities. An interactive quiz about paper recycling, recent news releases, and research reports are also available on the site, as well as a link to sign up for e-mail updates and information.

Basel Action Network (BAN)
c/o Earth Economics
206 First Ave. S., Ste. 410
Seattle, WA 98104
(206) 652-5555
website: www.ban.org

BAN is a nonprofit organization focused on confronting the global environmental injustice and economic inefficiency of toxic trade (toxic wastes, products, and technologies) and its devastating impacts. The group actively promotes sustainable and just solutions to the consumption and waste crises, banning waste trade while promoting green, toxic-free, and democratic design of consumer products. BAN's web page gathers up-to-date e-waste news articles from a variety of international sources and offers a photo gallery, reports, speeches, and links to dozens of other sites.

Bureau of International Recycling (BIR)
24 Avenue Franklin Roosevelt
1050 Brussels, Belgium
website: www.bir.org
e-mail: bir@bir.org

Founded in 1948, the BIR was the first federation to support the interests of the recycling industry on an international scale. Today the BIR represents over 750 member companies from the private sector and forty national associations in more than seventy countries. The federation provides a forum for its members to share their knowledge and experience. It serves as a platform to establish successful business relations and to promote recycling among other industrial sectors and policy makers. The BIR website provides statistics and other facts about recycling, as well as reports, brochures, newsletters, and posters.

Center for Ecological Technology (CET)
112 Elm St.
Pittsfield, MA 01201
(413) 445-4556
website: www.cetonline.org

Since 1976 the nonprofit CET has engaged in work that demonstrates and promotes practical, affordable solutions to the environmental challenges encountered in our daily activities. The CET's mission is to research, develop, demonstrate, and promote those technologies that have the least disruptive impact on the natural ecology of the earth. The website offers online publications about recycling, composting, and handling of hazardous materials, as well as links to other information and organizations. The CET publishes a quarterly online newsletter, *EcoBytes*.

Competitive Enterprise Institute (CEI)
1899 L St. NW, 12th Fl.
Washington, DC 20036
website: www.cei.org

The CEI is a nonprofit public policy organization dedicated to advancing the principles of limited government, free enterprise, and individual liberty. Its mission is to promote both freedom and fairness by making good policy good politics. The CEI addresses many issues on its website. Articles and reports about garbage and recycling include "Solid Waste Management," "Mandated Recycling of Electronics: Creating a Mountain Out of a Landfill," "Trash Counterproductive Waste Disposal Policies," and "Time to Recycle Recycling?"

Glass Packaging Institute (GPI)
700 N. Fairfax St., Ste. 510
Alexandria, VA 22314
(703) 684-6359
website: www.gpi.org/recycleglass

The GPI serves as the voice for the glass container industry in Washington, DC, and across the country. The GPI serves its member companies through legislative, public relations, promotional, and technical activities. Its website includes a comprehensive "Recycle Glass" section with information, fast facts, and frequently asked questions about recycling and the environment, community recycling, and bar and restaurant recycling.

Grist
710 Second Ave., Ste. 860
Seattle, WA 98104
(206) 876-2020
website: www.grist.org

Grist is a nonprofit environmental news, opinion, and humor organization supported by foundation grants, user contributions, and advertising. Calling itself "Grist: it's gloom and doom with a sense of humor," the organization uses the slogan "Laugh now—or the planet gets it." The website includes feature articles, blogs, columns, cartoons, and an advice column called "Ask Umbra" that addresses environmental topics that include recycling, electronic waste, composting, and the idea of a zero-waste future.

International Bottled Water Association (IBWA)
1700 Diagonal Rd., Ste. 650
Alexandria, VA 22314
(703) 683-5213
website: www.bottledwater.org/education/recycling

The IBWA is an authoritative source of information about all types of bottled waters. Founded in 1958, the IBWA's member companies include US and international bottlers, distributors, and suppliers. The organization's website includes a "Recycling" section, which presents facts about plastic bottles; news articles; and a series of videos, including "Recycling Empty Plastic Bottles," "College Bottled Water Ban," "The Adventures of Recycle Kitty," and more.

National Recycling Coalition
1220 L St. NW, Ste. 100–155
Washington, DC 20005
(202) 618-2107
website: http://nrcrecycles.org

The National Recycling Coalition is a national nonprofit advocacy group that works to support waste reduction and sound management practices for raw materials in North America, leading to an environmentally sustainable economy. Its three thousand members span all aspects of waste reduction, reuse, and recycling, including local recycling coordinators, state and federal regulators, corporate environmental managers, environmental educators, consumers, and waste management professionals. The website includes transcripts of webinar presentations such as "Organics—Food Waste Recycling—Does It Add Up?" and "New to You: A Webinar on the Environmental,

Economic, and Social Benefits of Reuse," as well as a recycling location search engine for consumers.

Natural Resources Defense Council (NRDC)
40 W. Twentieth St.
New York, NY 10011
(212) 727-2700
website: www.nrdc.org/recycling/default.asp

The NRDC was founded in 1970 by a group of law students and attorneys at the forefront of the environmental movement. NRDC lawyers helped write some of America's bedrock environmental laws. Today its staff of more than three hundred lawyers, scientists, and policy experts, supported by more than 1 million members and online activists, work to protect the planet's wildlife and wild places and to ensure a safe and healthy environment for all living things. The website's "Recycling 101" section gives tips for consumers; information about ocean pollution, electronic waste, and the recycling economy; and advice for businesses.

Recycling Works!
1958 University Ave.
Berkeley, CA 94704
website: www.recyclingworkscampaign.org

The Recycling Works! campaign brings together waste workers and community and environmental justice activists to create recycling programs that generate good jobs, combat climate change, create energy independence, and revitalize community health. The campaign was initiated by the International Brotherhood of the Teamsters and the Global Alliance for Incinerator Alternatives. The website collects news articles, graphs and charts, policy recommendations, and reports, including *More Jobs, Less Pollution: Growing the Recycling Economy in the U.S.*

Steel Recycling Institute (SRI)
25 Massachusetts Ave. NW, Ste. 800
Washington, DC 20001
website: www.recycle-steel.org

The SRI is an industry association that promotes and sustains the recycling of all steel products. The SRI educates the solid waste industry, government, businesses, and consumers about the benefits of steel's infinite recycling cycle. The website offers educational materials for teachers and community leaders, ranging from a video for prekindergarten children to "Cycles for Science," a high school curriculum focusing on recycling, solid waste management, and natural resource management. Other information, intended for industry workers and policy makers, includes up-to-date statistics and trends.

For Further Reading

Books

Fishman, Charles. *The Big Thirst: The Secret Life and Turbulent Future of Water*. New York: Free Press, 2011. This is a sweeping look at how humans use water for nourishment, recreation, and cleanliness, as well as how new technologies can help bring fresh, clean water to all who need it.

Gleick, Peter H. *Bottled and Sold: The Story Behind Our Obsession with Bottled Water*. Washington, DC: Island, 2010. Gleick, a freshwater scientist, explains how consumers came to believe that bottled water is cleaner and safer than tap water, as well as the economic and environmental consequences of that misconception.

Hahn, Leon. *Municipal Solid Waste in the U.S.: Facts, Trends and Perspective*. New York: Nova Science, 2011. This volume gathers more than thirty years of data from the US Environmental Protection Agency and other sources, highlighting trends in what is collected and recycled.

Hohn, Donovan. *Moby-Duck: The True Story of 28,000 Bath Toys Lost at Sea and of the Beachcombers, Oceanographers, Environmentalists, and Fools, Including the Author, Who Went in Search of Them*. New York: Viking, 2011. Woven through the story of his own adventurous travels, the author explains the science behind ocean currents, plastic manufacture and disintegration, and how the world creates and discards plastic trash.

Hugo, Pieter. *Permanent Error*. New York: Prestel USA, 2011. Photographer Hugo documents one garbage dump in Ghana where untrained and unprotected workers use dangerous methods to remove precious materials from discarded computers.

Humes, Edward. *Garbology: Our Dirty Love Affair with Trash*. New York: Avery, 2012. A Pulitzer Prize–winning writer explains where trash comes from and what happens to it. The author interviews sanitation workers, scientists, artists, and a family that throws away less than one bagful of trash every year.

Jensen, Derrick, and Aric McBay. *What We Leave Behind*. New York: Seven Stories, 2009. In this book, a writer and an activist argue that the core of living sustainably must be the idea that one being's waste must always become another being's food.

MacBride, Samantha. *Recycling Reconsidered: The Present Failure and Future Promise of Environmental Action in the United States*. Cambridge, MA: MIT Press, 2012. Using case studies to demonstrate the inadequacies of modern attempts to reuse and recycle, MacBride raises broad questions about how waste should be handled locally, nationally, and internationally.

Pritchett, Laura, ed. *Going Green: True Tales from Gleaners, Scavengers, and Dumpster Divers*. Norman: University of Oklahoma Press, 2009. This volume is a collection of twenty essays by people on the edge of reusing and recycling: those who eat road kill, recycle their waste water, and find treasures and necessities by Dumpster diving.

Schendler, Auden. *Getting Green Done: Hard Truths from the Front Lines of the Sustainability Revolution*. New York: PublicAffairs, 2009. Schendler argues that the small changes that consumers and small businesses are making to make their lives "greener" actually have little effect on solving big environmental problems.

Zimring, Carl A. *Cash for Your Trash: Scrap Recycling in America*. Piscataway, NJ: Rutgers University Press, 2009. Zimring, a historian, traces the practical, social, economic, and environmental concerns that have influenced scrap recycling as far back as the colonial period.

Periodicals and Internet Sources

Belli, Brita. "Fairness in Waste," *E:The Environmental Magazine*, March–April, 2011.

Bhanoo, Sindya N. "New York State Cracks Down on E-waste," *New York Times*, June 7, 2010.

Bridgers, Leslie. "A Waste of Time? Recycling Is Anything But," *Portland (ME) Press Herald*, November 10, 2011.

Brown, Lester R. "Reduce, Reuse, Recycle, Rethink," *Mother Earth News*, August–September 2009.

Burton, Susan. "Recycling? Fuhgeddaboudit," *Mother Jones*, May–June 2009.

Castillo, Michelle. "Electronic Waste: Where Does It Go and What Happens to It?," *Time*, January 14, 2011.

Chertow, Marian. "The Ecology of Recycling," *UN Chronicle*, Special Climate Issue, 2009.

Considine, Mary-Lou. "Negotiating the National E-waste Mountain," *ECOS*, June–July 2009.

Doucette, Kitt. "The Plastic Bag Wars," *Rolling Stone*, August 4, 2011.

Elgin, Ben, and Brian Grow. "The Dirty Secret of Recycling Electronics," *Business Week*, October 27, 2008.

Fishman, Charles. "Message in a Bottle," *Fast Company*, July 1, 2007.

Ghosh, Jayati. "Our Techno Culture Is Creating Dangerous Digital Dumps," *Triple Crisis*, December 7, 2011.

Goffman, Ethan. "E-Waste Not: Recycling Our High-Tech Cast-Offs," *E: The Environmental Magazine*, September–October 2011.

Gugliotta, Guy. "Retiring Tires: A Heated Debate on Using Them as Fuel," *Discover*, February 2008.

Hannum, William H., Gerald E. Marsh, and George S. Stanford. "Risky Recycling?," *Scientific American*, September 2008.

Hatch, David. "High Tech, Low Standards," *National Journal*, April 28, 2011.

Hickman, Leo. "The Truth About Recycling," *Guardian* (Manchester, UK), February 25, 2009.

Hutchinson, Alex. "Is Recycling Worth It? *PM* Investigates Its Economic and Environmental Impact," *Popular Mechanics*, November 13, 2008.

Jensen, Derrick. "Bright Green Reality Check," *Orion*, November–December 2011.

Jozefowicz, Chris. "Waste Woes," *Current Health 2*, January 2010.

Kapur, Akash. "Drowning in a Sea of Garbage," *New York Times*, April 22, 2010.

Kaufman, Rachel. "Seeking a Safer Future for Electricity's Coal Ash Waste," National Geographic News, August 15, 2011. www .nationalgeographic.com

Lantz, Daniel. "Mixed Residuals," *Resource Recycling*, December 2008.

Linnell, Jason. "The E-waste Disconnect," *Waste Age*, May 1, 2010.

Maqueda, Manuel. "The Bioplastic Labyrinth," *Earth Island Journal*, Autumn 2010.

Meacham, Jon. "Recycling Won't Save Us, but Greed Might," *Newsweek*, November 9, 2009.

Motavalli, Jim. "Waste Not," *E: The Environmental Magazine*, March–April 2011.

Rubinstein, Lynn. "Whatever Happened to Mandatory Recycling?," *Resource Recycling*, November 2011.

Wagner, Gernot. "Going Green but Getting Nowhere," *New York Times*, September 7, 2011.

Walsh, Bryan. "E-waste Not," *Time*, January 19, 2009.

Zeller, Jr., Tom. "Recycling: The Big Picture," *National Geographic*, January 2008.

Websites

Center for Sustainability at Aquinas College (www.centerforsustain ability.org). A web-based clearinghouse of information for consumers, businesspeople, nonprofit organizations, students, and governmental agencies interested in sustainable practices.

Earth911.com (http://earth911.com). Easy-to-read information about the basics of recycling various common materials, a collection of news articles, and lists of recyclers across the United States, searchable by zip code.

Environmental Industry Associations Solid Waste Information, Publications and Resources (www.environmentalistseveryday.org /publications-solid-waste-industry-research/index.php). A large collection of reports, fact sheets, articles, and opinion pieces, with a special section for teachers and students.

Grinning Planet (www.grinningplanet.com). Humor and information about health, energy, and environmental issues through articles, cartoons, videos, and audio.

Landfill Site (www.landfill-site.com/index.html). A collection of useful information—including articles, photos, and a glossary—about waste management, concentrating on landfills, landfilling, and waste management engineering in the United Kingdom.

Learn the Issues: Waste (www.epa.gov/gateway/learn/wastes.html). Sponsored by the US Environmental Protection Agency, offering comprehensive and reliable material on nonhazardous and hazardous waste, composting, and recycling for professional researchers, consumers, and students.

Index

Hazardous waste, 22–23
  household, 13–14
High-density polyethylene
  (HDPE), 103
Hill, Jean, 80
Hugo, Pieter, 73

I
Incineration
  can produce clean energy,
    26–31
  energy generated by, 29
  produces pollution/produces
    little energy, 32–39
  See also Waste-to-energy
    plants
Ingenthron, Robin, 67

J
Jobs
  from incineration *vs.*
    recycling, 36
  recycling creates, 49

K
Kaplan, Melanie D.G., 93
King, Leslie, 68

L
Landfills, *24*
  are convenient/
    environmentally safe,
    11–19
  are not good long-term
    solution, 20–25
  gases leaked from, 24

numbers of, 14
prevalence of leaks in, 22
recycling reduces pressure on,
  51–52
Lantz, Daniel, 59
Lead, 31
  in cathode ray tubes, 68–69
  hazards of, 75
Liquid pollutants (leachate), 25
  collection from landfills, 12
Love Canal (NY), 23

M
McCarthy, Deborah, 68
McClain, Steven, 8
Menning, Reo, 61, 62
Mercury, emissions of, 34
Methane (CH_4), 24–25
  from biomass, 29
  recycling reduces emissions
    of, 50
Mikolajczyk, Lawrence, 63–65
Mining
  of virgin metals, 70–71
  waste from, 21
Mobro garbage barge, 42, *43*
Morawski, Clarissa, 54
Municipal solid waste (MSW)
  composition of, 22
  generation rates for, *23*
  packaging reduces production
    of, 42–44
  per capita production of, 8,
    21, 28
  percentage of total biomass
    energy produced from, 28

plastic, bioplastics can reduce, 93–98
sources of, *17, 21*

N
Natural Resources Defense Council, 44
Navarro, Mireya, 8
New York City, reduction in curbside recycling in, 8
New York Times (newspaper), 8
North Carolina, economic benefits of recycling in, 52

O
Obama, Barack, 96
O'Connor, Mary Catherine, 99
Office of Technology Assessment, US (OTA), 44–45
Osibanjo, Oladele, 76–77
OTA (Office of Technology Assessment, US), 44–45

P
Packaging, reduces total waste production, 42–44
Paper, recycled, percentage usable *vs.* contaminated, *58*
Particulate pollution, 34–35
from waste-to-energy plants, 38
Pay-as-you-go systems, 44
Pennsylvania, benefits of recycling in, 53
Permanent Error (Hugo), 73

PET. *See* Polyethylene terephthalate
PLA (polylactic acid), 102, 103, 104
PlantBottle, 94–96, 98, 100
problems with recycling of, 104
Plastic beverage bottles, number disposed per hour in US, 82
Plastic beverage bottles, PET percentage recycled, 102
sources of, *89*
Pollution
recycling contributes to, 44–46
waste incineration produces, 32–39
Polyethylene terephthalate (PET), 94, 96, 102, 103, 104
sources of bottles made from, *89*
Polylactic acid (PLA), 102, 103, 104
Property and Environment Research Center, 41
Puckett, Jim, 73–74, 75, 76

R
Rademacher, Michael, 7
Recyclable materials
contamination of, 57, *58*
markets for, 7
Recycled materials, single-stream recycling yields less useful, 54–59
Recycling/recycling programs

Picture Credits

© Mary Andrews/Alamy, 83

© AP Images/David Bookstaver, 43

© AP Images/Mike Derer, 56

© AP Images/Steve Helber, 101

© avatra images/Alamy, 13

© Caro/Alamy, 74

© Phil Degginger/Alamy, 40

© Mark Dye/Newscast/Landov, 95

© Gale/Cengage Learning, 17, 23, 30, 37, 58, 63, 70, 77, 84, 89, 97

© Clynt Garnham Environmental/Alamy, 35

© incamerastock/Alamy, 24

© Ian Miles-Flashpoint Pictures/Alamy, 51

© Marcus Mok/Alamy, 64

© Martin Shields/Alamy, 28

© Jeff Smith/Alamy, 10

© Nathan Smith/Alamy, 90

© Tiit Veermae/Alamy, 79